THE
LEADER
LAB

THE
LEADER
LAB

Core Skills to Become
a Great Manager, *Faster*

THE
LEADER
LAB

Tania Luna
LeeAnn Renninger, PhD
Co-Founders of LifeLabs Learning

WILEY

Published by John Wiley & Sons, Inc., Hoboken, New Jersey.
Published simultaneously in Canada.

For general information on our other products and services or for technical support, please contact our Customer Care Department within the United States at (800) 762-2974, outside the United States at (317) 572-3993 or fax (317) 572-4002.

Wiley also publishes its books in a variety of electronic formats. Some content that appears in print may not be available in electronic formats. For more information about Wiley products, visit our web site at www.wiley.com.

Library of Congress Cataloging-in-Publication Data:

ISBN: 9781394331703 (Paperback)
ISBN: 9781119793335 (ePub)
ISBN: 9781119793328 (ePDF)

Cover Design: Wiley
Cover Image: © Valeriya_Dor/Shutterstock

SKY10097564_013125

This book is dedicated to our Labmates: the brilliant, playful, strange, and passionate catalysts at LifeLabs Learning who help people master life's most useful skills every day.

Contents

The Backstory

Let's face it: great managers are rare, and *becoming* a great manager can take many (difficult) years. But what if there were a way to simplify the complexity of leadership, and become a great manager faster? There is a way to do just that, and we've written this book to show you how. The skills we'll share with you aren't hard, but they do require deliberate practice. As you master each skill, you'll notice your life getting easier, and you'll see yourself making a bigger difference in the world, every day. But first let's talk about why managers matter.

Why Managers Matter

Here's the bad news: 88% of people say they are relieved when their manager is out sick (Leone 2020). Worldwide, only 20% of employees strongly agree they are managed in a motivating way. Poor management costs roughly $7 trillion globally every year in terms of errors, inefficiencies, and turnover – not to mention people's mental and physical health (Wigert and Harter 2017). If you've ever had a bad manager, you've experienced firsthand how it can turn joyful work into daily dread.

There. Now that that's out of the way, let's spend the rest of this book together dwelling on the good news. Great managers make work and life better. They help teams achieve amazing results. They help individuals do their life's best work. We (Tania and LeeAnn) have seen this time and time again thanks to the work we do through our company, LifeLabs Learning, where we train hundreds of thousands of employees at innovative companies around the world, including Google, Warby Parker, the *New York Times*, Yale, TED, Sony Music, and over 1,000 others.

Our workshop participants told us countless stories of managers who changed their lives. There was Marta, whose team members said she helped them bring their real selves to work for the first time in their careers. There was John, who celebrated every milestone his team reached with such consistency that people said it taught them to be better parents. There was Bernardo, who helped lead a company from near extinction to success. There was Niko, who helped her team members keep updating their résumés so they could see how much they'd grown. And there were so many others. We saw that great managers had infinite ripple effects at work and in life, so we made it our mission to help more people become great managers *faster*.

Sure, folks can learn on the job, but experience is a slow and confusing teacher. We can't afford to sit around and wait for leadership skills to kick in. There are too many costs and too many people at stake.

Can someone really learn to be a better manager? You bet. Just as in any profession, from medicine to music, some people find some skills easier than others. We don't recommend that everyone be a manager, just as we don't recommend that everyone be a ballet dancer. But everyone can become a better manager faster by applying the lessons in this book.

How do we know? When we follow up with managers we've trained at LifeLabs Learning three months and one year later, over 90% say they are still applying the skills they've learned and are better managers as a result. Our clients report an increase in manager effectiveness, employee engagement, and company productivity. Our favorite part? Our workshop participants tell us that becoming better managers has also helped them become better versions of themselves.

What a Manager Is (Today)

Before we get into the skills of great managers, let's align on what a manager is in today's workplace. The etymology of the word "manager" is actually pretty cringeworthy. It comes from the term "to handle," especially tools or horses. The dehumanizing implication is that people are resources to be managed. This way of thinking created efficiencies when craftspeople became factory workers, and managers had to ensure uniformity and predictability. Thinking was the manager's role, while doing was the responsibility of the workers.

As you know, things are different now. Given the growing rate of change and competition, companies today rely on *everyone* collaborating, communicating, learning, and innovating. Unlike the original managers who had to limit people's thinking, today's managers have to help people think faster and better. The best managers no longer manage people. They manage resources, processes, time, priorities, and even themselves. They *catalyze* results rather than control behavior. They help their team members achieve what neither the manager nor the team members could achieve alone.

The long-debated distinction between leaders and managers is also growing obsolete. It used to be said that leaders handled the unknown, while managers handled predictable work. It was once believed that leaders guide others through influence, while managers control through authority. While leaders don't have to be managers, nowadays managers must be leaders. For this reason, we'll use the terms "manager" and "leader" interchangeably throughout this book and equip you with skills to manage and lead well. So, if you want to become a great manager faster, where should you start?

The Surprising Skills That Matter Most

Great Managers, Assemble!

Consider this: in a 10-minute exchange with one person, a manager uses hundreds of words, microexpressions, and gestures. Which of these behaviors result in a team member who's productive and engaged and which result in the opposite? When we began our mission to help people become great managers faster, we couldn't separate the signal from the noise. So we thought back to the Martas, Johns, Bernardos, and Nikos. We wondered: can we learn directly from these leadership legends? Thanks to this insight, we assembled our first group of research participants.

At LifeLabs Learning, we had the unique opportunity of training people at many different companies around the world. So, every time we went into a company to lead workshops, we asked, "Who here is a great manager?" The people who were named again and again had the most engaged teams and a track record of achieving results. We also compared these "greats" with average managers. Our initial plan was to conduct interviews with the greats and the average, and look for differences in their answers. To make a long story short, this approach was mostly . . . a flop. When we asked managers which behaviors led to their success, the answers of the great and average folks were not predictive of performance. For example, guess which type of manager (average or great) most often said, "I think it's important to be a good listener."

The answer? Nearly every manager talked about the importance of listening. So what actually made the greats different? We interviewed the managers' teams to see if we could gather more helpful data. This approach yielded some interesting insights. For example, we learned there was no correlation between managers believing they were good listeners and their team members rating them as good listeners. But we were still no closer to understanding the behaviors that distinguished great managers.

What's in the Black Box?

You see, one of the challenges with studying management is that it is a uniquely private practice. Nearly all exchanges happen behind closed doors, whether physical or virtual. So, as our next plan of action, we wanted to see if managers would open their doors to us. We asked if we could watch them share feedback, lead meetings, and give pep talks. We wanted to recreate the "black box" of the aviation world – the recording device that has enabled countless improvements in flight crew dynamics. Surprisingly, many said yes. (And to them, we are eternally grateful.) As a result, we got to sit in on one-on-ones and team meetings, as well as solo working sessions where we asked managers to "think out loud" as they made complex decisions. With the black box open, we were able to observe their behaviors in action.

When we began our research on what makes great managers different, we started with the implicit premise that it is the big behaviors that count. Without realizing it, we were waiting for something cinematic to happen. We wanted to get goosebumps and imagine an orchestral crescendo while hearing an inspiring speech. What we found instead were behaviors so small we barely noticed them. But there they were, distinctly standing out again and again in the "black boxes" of the great managers. Even though these leaders came from different industries, professions, and cultures, they had a small set of small behaviors in common.

Discovering Behavioral Units

We've come to call each small behavior we observed a Behavioral Unit (or BU for short). No, they are not dramatic, but they are so elegant in their simplicity that they do give us goosebumps. We began to spot them in casual conversations, in times of conflict, and in every meeting. Even in the midst of our own debates about what makes great managers different, we'd stop one another and say, "Hey, nice BU!" Now that these BUs were visible to us, they were impossible to unsee. Once you learn them, you too will start to spot them everywhere.

The Manager Core: Your Leadership Swiss Army Knife

Once we learned how important BUs are, we thought we had our research breakthrough. Then, we realized something even more exciting: not all BUs are created equal. While great managers exhibit dozens of BUs, there is a foundational set of seven that come up in more contexts than any other. We call these the Core BUs. They are the small but mighty behaviors we will focus on in **Part I** of this book. What are these tiny champions of the leadership world? We are proud to present each one, chapter by chapter:

> **Chapter 1:** Q-step
> **Chapter 2:** Playback
> **Chapter 3:** Deblur
> **Chapter 4:** Validate
> **Chapter 5:** Linkup
> **Chapter 6:** Pause
> **Chapter 7:** Extract

Once you are familiar with the Core BUs, you will be ready to graduate to **Part II** of this book, which is based on our most popular workshops at LifeLabs Learning. In each chapter, we will show you how to string various BUs together to form the eight Core *Skills* of great managers.

While BUs are micro-behaviors, skills are packages of different BUs and tools mixed together to help you handle an even broader range of obstacles and opportunities. As an analogy, think of knowing the alphabet as a BU and of writing as a skill. Based on our manager research, we found that, just as not all

BUs are created equal, not all skills are equally versatile. So, in Part II, we'll bring you only the skills we refer to as the "tipping point skills." These are the skills that "tip" over into the widest number of domains, making the biggest impact in the shortest time. What are these famed Core Skills? Drum roll please . . . the skills you will be learning throughout Part II of this book are:

Chapter 8: Coaching Skills
Chapter 9: Feedback Skills
Chapter 10: Productivity Skills
Chapter 11: Effective One-on-Ones
Chapter 12: Strategic Thinking
Chapter 13: Meetings Mastery
Chapter 14: Leading Change
Chapter 15: People Development

Think of the Core BUs as your leadership Swiss Army knife. A single Swiss Army knife has a small set of tools, and yet this finite set alone will let you open canned foods, start a fire, make repairs, defend yourself, trim your nails, remove splinters, and infinite other things. In the same way, the Core BUs will get you through just about any leadership challenge and fit neatly into the pocket of your memory. Each time you learn how to use different Swiss Army knife tools to achieve a result, you learn a new skill. That's what the Core Skills throughout this book will help you do: rapidly combine different BUs and tools to become a great manager faster.

Your Leader Lab

So, let's get into it. We'll now move away from our telescopic view of managers and saunter over to the microscope. We'll zoom in on the specific behaviors of great managers, sharing behavioral science research along the way. But this deep dive into research is not the only reason this book is called *The Leader Lab*. Yes, we will bring you lessons from our laboratory and from leadership labs across the world, but the most important lab we will focus on is *yours*.

The very best managers we studied were all wildly different, but one thing they had in common was a practice of constantly experimenting. Rarely did they mention that their leadership skills came naturally to them. On the contrary, most confessed that they made countless mistakes on a regular basis. They just weren't content to leave their mistakes in the past. Instead, much like world-class chess masters, they "replayed" their days, noticing what they did well, where they went wrong, and what new leadership experiments they can try out in the future. In this way, they became the directors of their own leader labs. They turned every interaction into a learning opportunity and became great managers faster. And so, we now invite you to put on your lab coat and enter your personal leader lab. Don't just read this book. Use it as your guide to experiment, reflect, and accelerate your manager mastery.

Not only will the Manager Core help you become a better catalyst of progress for your team, but it will also make your life easier. We began this chapter by pointing out how hard it is to have a bad manager, but actually *being* a manager is even harder. Feeling responsible for that combination of company results and people's needs, hopes, fears, and dreams can be a heavy weight to carry – especially when there is never enough time and no one to help you figure things out. As a manager, you will face some of the toughest challenges of your life. While the BUs and skills we share with you will make your ride to manager mastery no less wild, we promise to make it more fun, rewarding, and a lot faster.

How to Use This Book

As You Read

The first time you read this book, we recommend you move through it from beginning to end, since lessons in each chapter carry through to all chapters that follow. Don't read passively like you're sitting in on a lecture. After all, this is a lab. *Actively* reflect on your own behaviors along the way. Ask yourself:

- "Do I do this?"
- "What might I try doing differently?"
- "When can I try it?"

When an insight strikes, pause to jot it down in the margins. For even faster learning, summarize the key points you learned, and share them with your manager, your team, your cat, or anyone willing to listen. Research shows that we learn faster by teaching, a handy phenomenon known as the "protégé effect" (Chase et al. 2009).

Mia the Manager

Throughout the book, you'll get to see leadership in action, much like we got to do through our research. In each chapter, you'll listen in on conversations with a manager named Mia (a composite of our research participants) as she navigates the ups and downs of her role. Mia is a first-time manager with a common story: she's inexperienced, overwhelmed, and determined to do a good job. There's just one thing about Mia that is decidedly *un*common. She has a magic Do-Over Button. That's right. While the great managers we studied "replayed" their management moments in their minds, Mia has the unique advantage of going back in time to try again.

"Wait, time travel?" you might be saying. "Why introduce one of the most notoriously complex plot devices into a book on leadership skills?" Well, for starters, because this might be the only chance we get to publish sci-fi. But more importantly, because people's brains learn best through observation. By following Mia's story and hearing the contents of her team's "black box," you'll get to spot common leadership mistakes in real time, see each BU and skill in action, and strengthen your own management muscles. Along the way, we encourage you to travel back to instances in your own past where you succeeded or stumbled as a manager, and bring experiment ideas back to the future for your personal leader lab.

Practice Stations

Distributed throughout each chapter, you'll also see "Practice Stations," as you would in a physical laboratory. Spend some time at these stations to rapidly transform your insights into habits. These stations are an opportunity to test out what you've learned and collect brain-friendly tips to help the learning stick in your memory.

Bonus: For live practice and real-time feedback, visit leaderlab.lifelabslearning.com.

Your Lab Reports

At the end of each chapter, you'll have a personal Lab Report to complete that will prompt you to do the following:

1. Extract your takeaways from the chapter so you can easily return to them later.
2. Assess your current competence level to increase your self-awareness.
3. Select a small experiment from a bank of ideas to try in your own leader lab.
4. Extract your learnings once you have tried out the experiment to accelerate your learning.

Bonus Inclusion Stations

Because great leadership is synonymous with inclusive leadership, you'll also have access to bonus "Inclusion Stations" at leaderlab.lifelabslearning.com. Visit these Inclusion Stations for extra support in applying the lessons in this book to every member of your team, mitigating the impact of bias, and giving each person access to great leadership. You'll discover research and pro tips for cross-cultural collaboration, leading remote and distributed teams, as well as overall inclusion guidance. Why apply an inclusive lens to how you lead? Because teams are increasingly diverse, which means managers have to take deliberate action to leverage this diversity and overcome individual and systemic bias. Companies that harness the strength of their differences are more resilient, engaged, and see an average of 45% more revenue growth than their peers (Hewlett, Marshall, and Sherbin 2013).

Finally, give yourself an occasional fist bump or high five for your effort along the way. The world needs more great managers. Thank you for putting in the work to become an even better manager.

The Core BUs

R eady to enter Part I of the Leader Lab? In this first section, we'll equip you with the Core BUs, the small but powerful Behavioral Units that will immediately make your conversations, relationships, and decisions better:

1. Q-step

2. Playback

3. Deblur

4. Validate

5. Linkup

6. Pause

7. Extract

Once we introduce a BU, we will **bold** it every time we refer to it throughout the book and include its corresponding icon so it's easier to notice and faster for your brain to learn. Even when you're not reading, mentally **bold** these BUs when you spot them "in the wild." Each BU is a simple but versatile behavior you can notice and use every day, including the moment you put down this book.

Welcome to the Leader Lab.

1

Q-step

Let's begin by examining the first Behavioral Unit (BU) that stood out in our research on what makes great managers different. Imagine you joined us in the lab. You take a seat in a small, dark room behind a two-way mirror and observe a manager in a one-on-one meeting. You switch on your handy stopwatch and let it run for 15 minutes. During this time, you count every question the manager asks. Once time's up, you tally the results. What's your prediction? In the span of 15 minutes, how many questions does an average manager ask? How many questions does a great manager ask?

If you guessed 2 questions for average and 10 for great, you are exactly right. Great managers ask 5 times more questions. Not only does question quantity set great managers apart, it's also a marker of great negotiators, influencers, creative thinkers, and even the secret to getting a second date (Huang et al. 2017). In one study of over 519,000 calls, researchers found that the best salespeople also asked more questions (Orlob 2017). Of course, it's possible to ask terrible questions. ("What were you thinking?" and "How can you be so bad at this?" are definitely questions, and definitely not questions we recommend.) Question *quality* is essential (more on that in Chapter 8), but the necessary starting point is question *quantity*. Great managers simply ask more questions than average. In fact, before they go into "Telling Mode," they default to "Questions Mode." Their first step is to ask at least one question. We call this BU the "**Q-step**."

How does the **Q-step** BU help you become a great manager faster? Let's see its impact in action. We're going to join Mia in her first week as a manager. For context, she is excited about the role but also somewhat intimidated by the challenge of being Luca's manager. She and Luca both applied for the role, and he has more subject matter expertise than Mia. This is their first conversation since they got the news:

Version 1

Luca: Weird, right? Having different roles all of a sudden.
Mia: Yeah, but I'm excited. I hope you're okay with it.
Luca: Yep. It's all good. I don't even know if I wanted the job.
Mia: I don't want it to be any different between us. You know?
Luca: Yep.
Mia: I want to make process improvements that benefit all of us, like the stuff we've all been frustrated about.
Luca: Yep. Good. Well, I have to get back to work.
Mia: Oh, sure. Good talk.

Mia leaves the conversation feeling shaken. She tried to show care, but Luca seemed to grow more distant. Mia decides it's time to use her magic Do-Over Button. Let's see her try it again, leaning on the power of the **Q-step**:

Version 2: Do-Over

Luca: Weird, right? Having different roles all of a sudden.
Mia: Yeah. <u>How are you feeling about it?</u>
Luca: I feel fine . . . I guess.
Mia: <u>Would you be willing to share more of what's on your mind?</u>
Luca: Well . . . I'm happy for you, but, you know, I've been here longer. I'm not even sure if I wanted the job, but it sucks not to get it.

> **Mia:** Yeah. I hear you. I'm curious: <u>what did you like about the job description and what didn't you</u>? Maybe that can help us figure out how to make your current role better.
>
> **Luca:** Well, I didn't want to be responsible for everyone on the team hitting their goals. You can have that part! But I did like the idea of making process improvements.
>
> **Mia:** Oh, well . . . the truth is, you're better at many parts of this work than I am. I want to hear your ideas. <u>How can we add making process improvements into your role?</u>
>
> **Luca:** I'd like that. Maybe I could focus on one process to improve per quarter?
>
> **Mia:** Yes! I can set up a meeting for us to chat about it. <u>How does that sound?</u>
>
> **Luca:** That sounds good. Thanks. And Mia? Congratulations.

Phew. Good use of the Do-Over Button. Not only did Mia manage to ask 400% more questions, she also **Q-stepped**, making it more likely that Luca will keep making valuable contributions.

But Mia's day is just beginning. Next up, she sees her team member Olivia. Mia and Olivia have also been peers for several years, but Olivia has shown no interest in management. In fact, she seems to show less and less interest at work in general. So it catches Mia off guard when Olivia comes to her with a new idea:

Version 1

> **Olivia:** Hey, Mia. Now that you're our manager, maybe you could finally help us get the resources we need. I'd like to get an intern this summer. Can I do that?

Mia:	Oh, wow. The thing is, I know interns sound cheap, but they'll take up all your time.
Olivia:	We can use the internship program I was in back in the day. It's structured really well.
Mia:	Liv, it's never worth it. Trust me.
Olivia:	Okay . . . I guess I'll drop it.

For a moment, Mia feels great about this conversation. She helped Olivia avoid a big mistake. Then it hits her: she just wasted an opportunity to get Olivia reengaged at work. So, she presses the Do-Over Button:

Version 2: Do-Over

Olivia:	Hey, Mia. Now that you're our manager, maybe you could finally help us get the resources we need. I'd like to get an intern this summer. Can I do that?
Mia:	Thanks for coming to me with this! I definitely want to use this role to get us the resources we need. <u>What made you start thinking of getting an intern?</u>
Olivia:	I just never have enough time to finish everything on my plate.
Mia:	So that we could find the right solution, I'm curious: <u>what are you thinking you'd delegate to the intern, and what would that give you more time to do?</u>
Olivia:	Well, I guess I'm not even sure I know yet. It's unclear what my priorities should be.

What impact did you notice once Mia got a **Q-step** do-over? How about in general: what is the impact of asking questions before offering solutions?

Q-stepping Helps Managers Become More Effective Faster in at Least Three Ways

1. Q-stepping Helps You Diagnose the Underlying Problem Faster

In the conversation with Luca, we missed out on learning the source of his disappointment (not getting to make process improvements). And the conversation with Olivia got stuck in the binary (should we get an intern or not?) rather than uncovering her prioritization challenge. Just as a good physician would never prescribe medicine without first diagnosing the illness, a good manager cannot offer advice without first understanding the problem. Even though it might seem quicker to jump to a solution, a great solution to the wrong problem is still the wrong solution. The **Q-step** helps you diagnose faster, so it also helps you solve the right problem faster.

2. Q-stepping Helps You Develop People's Skills Faster

In her do-over conversations, Mia wasn't solving her team members' problems *for* them. Instead, her questions helped them clarify their thinking. The result? She also helped speed up problem-solving skill building they can apply to countless other situations. She was a catalyst. Without these developmental moments, managers become problem-solving bottlenecks, making it hard for the team to scale (and nearly impossible for the manager to take a vacation).

3. Q-stepping Lets You Catalyze Commitment

The "resolutions" in Mia's original conversations came with a heavy tax. She never learned about Luca's hopes, and Olivia left less likely to propose ideas in the future. As we'll share in more detail in Chapter 11, autonomy is at the heart of engagement. Research shows that when people play a leading role in solving their own problems, they shift from mere compliance – doing what they're told, into commitment – having the drive to achieve results (Deci and Ryan 2008).

So we know great managers ask more questions than average. But there is more to this finding. When we asked our research participants if asking questions came naturally to them, we were surprised to hear common answers like this:

> *"No! Solving problems comes naturally to me! Especially when I was a new manager, it actually felt painful to ask a question instead of jumping in with a good answer. I'd get so frustrated as I waited for my direct reports to figure things out on their own – especially when we were short on time."*

While a few managers said that questions were easy to ask, the majority reported at least some difficulty – with some answers bordering on suffering. This internal struggle makes sense. Most people become managers after they've had a stint as successful "makers." But the skillsets of these two roles are vastly different, much like the difference between soloists and conductors. Individual contributors succeed when they solve problems. Managers succeed when they *help* others solve problems.

When you transition from maker to manager, you have to learn to ignore the very instincts that made you successful in the past, *and* you have to deal with the delay of gratification that comes with waiting for others to achieve results. Most managers we interviewed understood that asking questions was essential, but they had to exercise restraint to change their problem-solving habits.

This push-pull of craving the instant gratification of giving an answer and wanting to invest in asking questions is oddly similar to the taxi driver study LeeAnn conducted at the University of Vienna. In cities across the world, taxi drivers honk horns. They honk to signal information, they honk to avoid danger, and they honk just because it feels good. It turns out that many taxi drivers honk even when they risk consequences like fines, angry drivers, and being stuck in traffic with a lot of other horn honkers. The solution to needless honking? Having the drivers label their "honk urge." As soon as they felt the need to honk, they called it out – a strategy referred to in psychology as "name it to tame it" (Lieberman et al. 2007). This simple intervention bought them just enough time to question whether honking was worth it.

Similarly, when we asked great managers to talk us through their thought process when someone came to them with a problem, we noticed that many trained themselves out of Telling Mode and into Questions Mode as their default. They still felt that honk urge, but they had established a new habit: ask at least one question before telling, or doing the **Q-step**.

Practice Station

Now that you've gotten to ride along through time with Mia, get some **Q-stepping** practice for yourself. Take a look at the following scenarios and decide how you would respond if you went into Telling Mode, then pivot to a **Q-step** by asking at least one question.

TELLING MODE	Q-STEP
Someone suggests an idea that has not worked in the past.	
Sample tell: That'll never work.	*Sample Q-step: What options have you considered? How did you decide on this one?*
Your manager tells you to cut your budget in half.	
Sample tell: I don't even have enough of a budget as it is!	*Sample Q-step: Can you share what led to the budget cut? What is it meant to achieve?*
Your coworker tells you your team members are difficult to work with.	
Sample tell: Yep, I think so too.	*Sample Q-step: What makes you say that? Would you share an example?*

 There are countless great questions you can **Q-step** with (we'll share some of our favorites throughout this book), but we are not suggesting that you travel so far back in time that you transform into Socrates. Remember how that turned out for him? The great managers we studied had plenty to say and said it often. The distinct BU that made them different is that they **Q-stepped** *before* telling, even if that meant asking just one question.

***

In summary: Notice when you have the urge to go into Telling Mode and switch into Questions Mode by **Q-stepping** (asking at least one question). Why? Questions help you diagnose the underlying problem, develop people's skills, and catalyze commitment. Now it's time to fill in your Lab Report so you can develop your **Q-step** habit faster. What do you think about that? (See what we did there?)

MY LAB REPORT	Today's Date:
My takeaways:	
I regularly Q-step before telling:	1　2　3　4　5　6　7　8　9　10 (strongly disagree)　(strongly agree)
Experiment idea bank:	• If someone asks me a question, then I'll Q-step by asking, *"What are your thoughts?"* • If I want to give advice, then I'll Q-step first. • If someone makes a suggestion I disagree with, then I'll Q-step.
One small experiment I'll try to increase my score by 1 point:	
Post-experiment Learning Extractions:	

Bonus: Want to take your manager skills to the next level? Check out the bonus Inclusion Stations at leaderlab.lifelabs-learning.com.

My Learning Tracker

1 out of 7 Core BUs collected. 0 of 8 Core Skills collected.

Q-step						

2

Playback

The next BU we stumbled upon in our research on what makes great managers different is a behavior that is so subtle we nearly missed it. We even doubted its significance until we realized it had also been identified as one of the most important BUs for a wide range of professionals, including physicians, psychologists, salespeople, consultants, lawyers, pilots, and hostage negotiators. This powerhouse BU goes by many names. At LifeLabs Learning, we call it the **"Playback."**

A **Playback** is a paraphrase of what you heard someone say. Why does it help you become a great manager faster? Take a look at the following conversation. We're now a few weeks into Mia's role as a manager, and Olivia is starting to open up about her challenges at work. Notice where **Playbacks** could have made it a better conversation:

Version 1

Olivia: Ugh. I'm avoiding my to-do list, and I'm not looking forward to our team project.

Mia: What do you think is going on?

Olivia: I don't know. I'm just kind of exhausted by everything lately.

Mia: Is it that you don't take breaks?

Olivia: I do, but I'm still tired.

Mia: When was the last time you took some time off to recharge?

Olivia: Well, I could use my vacation days, but then I'll be even more behind.

Mia: When would be better timing?

Olivia: I guess I could already set aside time in December when it's slower.

At first Mia is proud that she got to practice her question skills, but something felt off. She decides to hit her handy Do-Over Button to go back and **Playback**:

Version 2: Do-Over

Olivia: Ugh. I'm avoiding my to-do list, and I'm not looking forward to our team project.

Mia: Hmm. <u>Sounds like two things are on your mind: your to-do list and the project</u>. Right? Of those two, which is the bigger issue?

Olivia: That's right . . . . I guess the project is the bigger problem. It's really weighing on me because everyone is waiting for me to get it started.

Mia: <u>It's feeling like a lot of responsibility.</u>

Olivia: Right. I like having responsibility, but I don't want to let the team down.

Mia: <u>Okay, so it sounds like you want to be more confident about how to start</u>.

Olivia: Yeah. If the project starts well, the rest will probably go smoothly.

In both versions, Mia has good intentions. But while taking breaks and vacation days are lovely things to do (and we highly recommend them), this advice does little to solve the underlying problem that Olivia faces: figuring how to start that project. So, what is it about **Playbacks** that makes them so useful?

Playbacks Help Managers Make a Positive Impact Faster in Three Ways

1. Playbacks Create Clarity Faster

When someone comes to you with a problem, their thoughts are often a tangled web. This is especially the case when they are tinged with strong emotions. Using a **Playback** is a quick way to ensure you understand their problem. What's more, when people hear their words played back to them, it helps them simplify the complexity of their thoughts. Research has long shown that the mere act of talking out loud leads to faster problem-solving (Gagné and Smith Jr. 1962; Lupyan and Swingley 2011). Why? It's likely thanks to a neuropsychology hack called "spreading activation": as we start talking, our thoughts spread to different associations, drawing on more of our neural resources faster. Yes, fellow introverts, this even applies to us.

2. Playbacks Catch Misunderstandings Faster

Playbacks are also an efficient way to prevent misunderstandings. Hear an incorrect **Playback**? This is your chance to fix it before it becomes a problem. As a chilling example: a manager we interviewed told us about a $500,000 loss her company sustained within 24 hours because no one confirmed their understanding of the plan. One person assumed it was obvious they had to submit signed paperwork to their client, while the rest of the team assumed a verbal agreement was sufficient. (In case you're wondering, the paperwork was not optional.) "When I worked in carpentry, we always said, 'Measure twice, cut once,'" the manager told us. "After seeing a bunch of people almost lose their jobs over a miscommunication, I'll never forget that **Playbacks** are my 'measure twice' mechanism."

3. Playbacks Build Trust Faster

Playbacks provide instant confirmation of understanding. For us humans, being truly understood is one of the sweetest (and sadly, also rarest) psychological sensations. Understanding leads to faster trust-building, which results in people being more willing to share their thoughts and feelings with each other.

If the benefits of **Playbacks** sound soft and/or squishy, think of the hours of your life you've already lost to rambling conversations, unproductive conflict, team members avoiding tough conversations, and plain old misunderstandings. Life is too short to go another day without **Playbacks**. (Yep, that's how passionate we are about this BU.) So, how do you do a **Playback**? Here are a few different **Playback** types to try out:

PLAYBACK TYPES	
Content Playback	Play back the key information you heard. *Example: It sounds like you said _____. Did I get that right?*
Split-track	Play back and separate points when speakers bring up multiple topics. *Example: I think I heard two things: _____ and _____. Is that right?* *Which of those should we talk about first?*
Feelings Playback	Play back the feelings you sense the speaker is experiencing. *Example: Sounds like you're feeling _____.* *(excited, energized, motivated, hopeful, proud, connected, unsure, hurt, angry, left out, disappointed, sad, worried, insecure, stuck)*
Needs Playback	Play back the underlying need the speaker seems to have. *Example: So, it seems like what you're needing is more _____.* *(reassurance, connection, clarity, meaning, security, respect, recognition, trust, understanding, spontaneity, growth, freedom)*

PLAYBACK TYPES	
Playback pull	Ask someone to play back what you said to ensure understanding. *Example: I know I just said a lot. Would you mind playing back what we discussed to make sure we're seeing it the same way?*

Practice Station

To get some practice, try doing at least three different types of **Playbacks** with this message:

"I don't think this salary is right given the amount of experience I bring to the team. It's not like I'm just starting out in this role. I've been doing this work for many years. By now, I was hoping my title would demonstrate the leadership responsibilities I have on the team. It just doesn't seem fair."

Come up with your own responses before reading the samples below.

Sample Playbacks:

Split-track: Sounds like three things: the salary, the title, and the fairness of the situation.

Feelings: Sounds like you're feeling overlooked.

Needs: Sounds like you're needing a sense of respect and recognition.

While it may seem like using **Playbacks** will make conversations longer, they tend to lead to more efficient conversations in the short term *and* the long term. Take a look at the following interaction between Mia and Luca. No matter how hard Mia tries to ask questions, it doesn't quell Luca's frustration. The topic starts all over as though they are stuck in a conflict time warp. Try to spot where **Playbacks** could have helped move them forward:

Version 1

Luca: No one asked me for my perspective. Everyone's just rushing to do their own part.

Mia: What don't you like about how the project turned out?

Luca: The work ended up okay. Though if someone checked in with me, I would have told them this client prefers to see all the raw data, not the summary.

Mia: Okay, we can definitely send them the raw data. Thank you.

Luca: But in general, what's so hard about getting input early? I always involve others in client presentations. It's not hard.

Once the conversation finally ends, Mia realizes Luca wasn't ready for problem-solving. He needed to be heard first. She presses her Do-Over Button and tries again:

Version 2: Do-Over

Luca: No one asked me for my perspective. Everyone's just rushing to do their own part.

Mia: <u>Sounds like you want to be included in the process</u>.

Luca: Yes. Exactly.

Mia: I also want that. How about we build a check-in with you into the workflow?

Luca: Thanks for saying that. Yeah. I can put together an idea of how that would work.

Notice how swiftly even a touchy subject can get resolved with a well-placed **Playback**? Feeling unheard often leads people to repeat themselves again and again, sometimes in long, rambling monologues with enough plot twists to impress Agatha Christie. Once people know they are heard, they can shift their focus to finding a solution or simply accepting the situation.

Train your brain to spot **Playback** opportunities by observing another conversation, this time between Mia and her manager, Alex. As you observe their discussion, notice where your brain starts wanting a **Playback**:

Version 1

Mia: We can either prioritize hiring, or we can improve our onboarding process first. I'm worried if we don't focus on onboarding now, any new hire will take a while to become a solid contributor. But if we delay hiring, we might end up burning out the team.

> **Alex:** How are you hoping to improve the onboard-ing process?
>
> **Mia:** Well, we don't really have anything structured in place. I'd like to create a plan, but I just keep wondering what will happen if we put off hiring. Luca and Olivia are already really tired.
>
> **Alex:** Yeah, that's a good idea. I think we should definitely do that.
>
> **Mia:** Okay. Thanks for your support. That's where I'll start.

Pop quiz! What solution did Mia and Alex agree on? Even though Mia leaves the conversation energized, she soon realizes that she and Alex might have two totally different interpretations of the plan. Sensing a "managing up" moment, Mia hits the Do-Over Button:

Version 2: Do-Over

> **Alex:** How are you hoping to improve the onboard-ing process?
>
> **Mia:** Well, we don't really have anything structured in place. I'd like to create a plan, but I just keep wondering what will happen if we put off hiring. Luca and Olivia are already really tired.
>
> **Alex:** Yeah, that's a good idea. I think we should definitely do that.

Mia:	Okay. <u>And just to make sure we're aligned, it sounds like we agree that I should prioritize hiring over onboarding.</u> Is that how you see it too?
Alex:	Oh! I was actually agreeing that it makes sense to improve onboarding. But if you want to already start interviewing candidates that's also an option.
Mia:	<u>Okay, so it sounds like if I decide to prioritize hiring, I can move forward with it</u>.
Alex:	That's right. Thanks for clarifying.

When is it **Playback** time? You can use **Playbacks** whenever you sense any confusion in a conversation, when it sounds like someone is bringing up multiple topics at once, when it's important to be aligned, and when someone expresses strong emotions. As a bonus, **Playbacks** can also buy you time to calm down and think in the midst of a heated conversation.

Sounds like we're done with Chapter 2. Just for fun: **Play back** the key points of this chapter before looking at the summary. (And yes, that is our idea of fun.) See how well you did.

***

In summary: A **Playback** is a repeat or a paraphrase of what you heard someone say. Use **Playbacks** to create clarity, prevent misunderstandings, and build trust faster.

MY LAB REPORT	Today's Date:
My takeaways:	

I regularly Play back what I hear:	1 2 3 4 5 6 7 8 9 10 (strongly disagree) (strongly agree)
Experiment idea bank:	▪ If I'm confused, then I'll do a Playback. ▪ If I hear multiple points, then I'll Split-track. ▪ If someone is upset, then I'll do a Playback.
One small experiment I'll try to increase my score by 1 point:	
Post-experiment Learning Extractions:	

Bonus: Want to take your manager skills to the next level? Check out the bonus Inclusion Stations at leaderlab.lifelabs-learning.com.

My Learning Tracker
2 out of 7 Core BUs collected. 0 of 8 Core Skills collected.

Q-step	Playback						

3

Deblur

What do you see in this image?

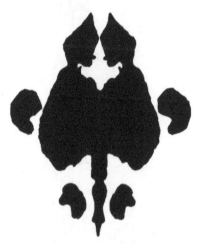

Source: Rorschach Inkblot Test, Pearson Scott Foresman. (Public Domain).

Don't worry. We're not testing you. Some folks see two people facing each other. Some see a crab. Some see lungs. Some see something entirely different. Which answer is right? Obviously, it's a crab. Just kidding – it's none of them. This is an intentionally ambiguous inkblot, meant to be open to interpretation. This inkblot-related insight will be obvious to anyone familiar with the Rorschach Test, but what wasn't obvious to us until we started studying the BUs of great managers is that conversations are splattered with inkblots – words that can be interpreted differently by different people. We at LifeLabs Learning have dubbed these "blur words." Some common examples include "better," "worse," "less," "more," and the ever-popular "as soon as possible."

Great managers are always on the lookout for blur words. They notice when people use them. They notice when they themselves use them. Then they apply the BU we've called **Deblur**. They turn ambiguous words into information that is clear enough for everyone to understand. Here are some sample **Deblurring** questions they ask.

Sample Deblurring Questions

- *What does _____ mean to you?*
- *Can you share an example?*
- *What's your definition of _____?*
- *What do you see as the impact of _____?*
- *How would we measure that?*
- *How would we know we've succeeded?*

Practice Station

Mia has decided to hire a new person, but getting input from her team members is harder than she expected. Take a look at the comment below about one of the candidates, and mentally (or physically) underline the blur words you spot:

I don't recommend hiring this candidate. She was closed-off and standoffish the entire time. The other candidates we interviewed were much warmer. I wouldn't even suggest inviting her to the next interview round. The other candidates were also much more qualified.

Which words in this example are blurry? Here are the biggest blur words:

I don't recommend hiring this candidate. She was <u>closed-off</u> and <u>standoffish</u> the <u>entire time</u>. The other candidates we interviewed were <u>warmer</u>. I wouldn't even suggest inviting her to the next interview round. The other candidates were also <u>more qualified</u>.

Notice how easy it could have been for Mia to leave the comment blurry and move onto the next candidate? Our brains are wired to fill gaps with snap interpretations. When we hear words like "standoffish," "warm," and "qualified," our brains make instant assumptions about what these words mean. We take for granted that we are talking about the same behaviors when, in reality, we might have vastly different meanings. For example, when we asked three people to **Deblur** a term as simple as "warm," we heard:

Deblurring "Warm": Three Distinct Definitions		
1. *They smile often and say complimentary things.*	**2.** *They listen closely and ask you questions.*	**3.** *They acknowledge people who helped them.*

How does **Deblurring** help managers become better faster?

Three of the Biggest Reasons Managers Benefit from Deblurring

1. Deblurring Prevents Miscommunication Faster

Blur words lead to misunderstandings of all shapes and sizes. Consider the experience of Sara, who got a frantic email from her manager (let's call him Sam). It went something like this: "Sara, the client needs the report by EOD. It's really time sensitive. Can you make it happen?"

The email came in at around 4 p.m. Sara knew the report would take hours to compile, and she had dinner plans with her cousin who was in town for just one night. Sara had been looking forward to dinner, but she was eager to make a good impression on Sam. So, she sighed, called her cousin to cancel, and spent the next four hours preparing the report. By the time she was finished, she was exhausted and hungry but proud. That is until she got fired the next morning. It turned out that neither Sam nor Sara **Deblurred** those three dangerous letters: *EOD*. To Sara, EOD meant End of her workday. To Sam and the client, EOD meant the end of the business day (5 p.m.). To this day, Sara shudders whenever someone uses that acronym.

2. Deblurring Improves Feedback Faster

One of the most frustrating and damaging types of feedback is blurry feedback. Blurry praise like "Great job!" misses out on a learning opportunity. (What was it that made the job great?) Worse yet, blurry critical feedback like "You didn't try hard enough" is pretty much guaranteed to trigger defensiveness. Great feedback is blur-word-free. We'll dig much deeper into feedback skills in Chapter 9, but for now, if you want to rapidly improve the quality of your feedback, start by **Deblurring** it.

3. Deblurring Improves Decision-Making Faster

One of the fastest ways to improve the quality of your decisions is to recognize how bias impacts your thinking. Bias is a preference for or against a person, group, or thing. Biases help people speed up their decisions, but biases (especially deeply ingrained biases around categories like ethnicity, race, gender, ability, age, class, sexual orientation, and religion) can also distort decisions – like hiring, firing, and promotion selections – without our conscious awareness. When you **Deblur,** you quickly increase your awareness of bias, leading to fairer and more thoughtful conclusions. For example, "What was it about that person that came across as unprofessional? What do you see as the impact?"

So how do you rapidly bulk up your **Deblurring** muscles? First and foremost, start mentally underlining the blur words you hear, read, and say. Recognition is the first step. When you notice other people's blur words, ask **Deblurring** questions. When you catch yourself getting blurry, stop and clarify. For example:

> *"This quarter our priority will be improving our customer service response time . . . . To Deblur what I mean by "improving" – the goal is to cut our response time in half, from an average wait time of 10 minutes to an average wait time of 5 minutes by the end of this quarter."*

Practice Station

Right now, describe someone you enjoy working with. What makes them a great coworker? Jot down your description below, underline each blur word you used, then convert them to specific language.

To hone the **Deblurring** BU faster, check back in with Mia's adventures in making her first hire:

Version 1

Mia:	So what did you both think of Kofi?
Luca:	I like that he brings a different professional background, but he wasn't a culture fit.
Mia:	Oh, really? What did you think, Liv?
Olivia:	Yeah, I agree. He was nice, but I think we need someone quicker on their feet.
Luca:	Right. He was friendly, but I also got the sense that he wasn't that interested in the job.
Mia:	Okay. Let's move onto the next candidate, I guess.

When the debrief ends, Mia is left with a nagging sense that they may be overlooking a terrific candidate. She remembers the team saying something about him not being a good "culture fit" and realizes she made an assumption about what that meant. So, Mia takes a deep breath and uses her Do-Over Button to go back in time and **Deblur**:

Version 2: Do-Over

Mia:	So what did you both think of Kofi?
Luca:	I like that he brings a different professional background, but he wasn't a culture fit.
Mia:	Hmm. <u>Can you share what you mean by "culture fit"</u>?
Luca:	He had low energy. To be honest, I couldn't even tell if he wanted the job.

Mia: Okay, so it sounds like two things: energy and interest. Is that right?

Luca: Yeah, I think so. Well . . . I guess I felt like he wasn't all that interested because of his energy. That's probably me jumping to a conclusion.

Olivia: I agree about his energy, though. He was just so mellow.

Mia: <u>Was it his talking speed</u>?

Olivia: A little bit. But he also took these long pauses before answering each question.

Mia: Got it. So he speaks slower than we do and pauses longer. <u>What do you see as the negative impact of that</u>?

Luca: Well, it makes me wonder about his sense of urgency.

Mia: <u>I think I know what you mean by "sense of urgency," but can you clarify so we're definitely talking about the same thing</u>?

Luca: Things like responding to problems quickly, meeting tight deadlines.

Mia: <u>Was there anything else from his interview that gave you the impression he doesn't have that sense of urgency</u>?

Luca: Well, no. Actually, he has a really impressive track record of getting things done. I don't know. Maybe it's just a cultural difference. We all grew up in New York City. He didn't.

Mia: Yeah. And on the flip side, I wonder if either of you can see a benefit to that difference?

Olivia: Well, yeah. Actually, it might be nice to have someone who makes us slow down and think things through before making a decision. We can go a little too fast sometimes.

This do-over conversation wraps up with a different conclusion. After **Deblurring** several other concerns as well as their positive reactions, the entire team agrees that Kofi is the right choice. What's more, they are all more confident in their decision because they took the time to **Deblur** and understand one another's perspectives. Mia can now make her very first job offer.

Later that day, Mia has another opportunity to practice her **Deblurring** BU when Luca vents to her about his career frustrations. Listen in and try to spot the blur words:

Version 1

Luca: It's just frustrating. I'm not growing in my career anymore.

Mia: Oof. That's not a good feeling.

Luca: I'm not trying to make you feel bad about the manager thing.

Mia: No, no. It's okay. This isn't about me. Is being a manager still one of your career goals?

Luca: I guess it should be. There aren't many other paths for me to take, and the manager job seems . . . interesting. Maybe I can be a manager if our department keeps growing.

Mia: I think that's realistic. Would it be helpful to come up with a plan for how you could prepare for that opportunity if or when it comes up?

Luca: Yeah, I guess that's the responsible thing to do.

They schedule a time to talk more, but then Mia notices that she's more enthusiastic about this plan than Luca is. Did she miss something blurry in the conversation? She decides to go back in time and try again, this time **Deblurring** the spots where she made assumptions:

> ## Version 2: Do-Over
>
> **Luca:** It's just frustrating. I'm not growing in my career anymore.
>
> **Mia:** I appreciate you talking to me about it. So we can figure this out together, I'm curious to hear: <u>what does "growing" mean to you?</u>
>
> **Luca:** I guess it means having new experiences. Learning new things. I think that's what was most interesting to me about the manager role.
>
> **Mia:** Yeah, I get that. And just to make sure we're talking about the same thing: <u>what's an example of something you *have* learned that felt good?</u>
>
> **Luca:** Hmm . . . Well, I had to learn about data visualization to be able to present our research. That was fun. I wish I had a lot more of those types of opportunities.
>
> **Mia:** <u>How do you picture "a lot more"?</u> In other words, <u>how often do you wish you were learning new things versus using the skills you already have?</u>
>
> **Luca:** I think having a new skill to work on every six months or so would be good.

***

In summary: Blur words are words that could mean different things to different people. Mentally underline blur words and ask **Deblurring** questions. Does it make sense to **Deblur** every ambiguous word you hear? "Good morning! Wait . . . what does 'good' mean to you?" No. Plenty of communication falls in the "clear enough" category. But when your goal is to give instructions, diagnose a problem, give or receive feedback, make a decision, delegate, or set a goal, **Deblurring** is the way to go. And by "way to go" we mean that you should definitely do it.

MY LAB REPORT	Today's Date:
My takeaways:	
I regularly Deblur unclear words:	1 2 3 4 5 6 7 8 9 10 (strongly disagree) (strongly agree)
Experiment idea bank:	▪ If I hear a blur word, then I'll ask a Deblurring question like *"What does _____ mean to you?"* ▪ If I use a blur word, then I'll Deblur myself. ▪ If I'm delegating, then I'll Deblur the request.
One small experiment I'll try to increase my score by 1 point:	
Post-experiment Learning Extractions:	

Bonus: Want to take your manager skills to the next level? Check out the bonus Inclusion Stations at leaderlab.lifelabs-learning.com.

My Learning Tracker

3 out of 7 Core BUs collected. 0 of 8 Core Skills collected.

Q-step	Playback	Deblur					

Validate

When we train managers to use the core BUs we've shared with you so far (**Q-step**, **Playback**, and **Deblur**), we see rapid behavior change, better results, and happier managers. After understanding these core concepts and doing practice drills in our workshops, managers become more inquisitive and precise in all their interactions. But there's one downside: overfocusing on clarity can start to come across as robotic. After all, we aren't just getting work done together – we are a bunch of emotional beings getting work done together. And work isn't just a series of tasks to cross off a list. Work is steeped in people's wildest dreams and deepest insecurities. So how can you breathe more care into your conversations faster? **Playbacks** help create emotional resonance, especially at the level of feelings and needs, but there is one other BU that's an essential addition to every manager's toolkit. Great managers "**Validate**."

Before we break down what **Validating** is, see if you notice what is *missing* from this conversation:

Version 1
Olivia: There's something that's been on my mind lately that's kind of hard to say.
Mia: Okay . . .
Olivia: I don't want to sound like I'm complaining, but the thing is, sometimes it's like I do all the grunt work around here, and then I'm invisible unless I make a mistake.
Mia: Okay. Sounds like what you're missing is a feeling of recognition.
Olivia: Well, yeah. But, I mean, I'm not saying I need a parade in my honor every time I meet a deadline. But a thank you would be nice sometimes. I know that's a weird request.
Mia: What would you want to see instead?

In this brief exchange, Mia is **Q-stepping**, doing **Playbacks**, and **Deblurring**. This is a *good* manager moment. But what would make it *great*? Mia has an idea. She uses her Do-Over Button, and gives it another try. Take a look at this exchange, this time, incorporating **Validations**:

Version 2: Do-Over

Olivia: There's something that's been on my mind lately that's kind of hard to say.

Mia: <u>I appreciate it when you bring up tough stuff with me. I always want to hear</u>.

Olivia. Thanks. I don't want to sound like I'm complaining, but the thing is, sometimes it's like I do all the grunt work around here, and then I'm invisible unless I make a mistake.

Mia: Oh, no. <u>I'm sorry to hear that</u>. <u>I want you to feel seen and appreciated</u>. It sounds like what you're missing is a feeling of recognition.

Olivia: Well, yeah. I'm not saying I need a parade in my honor every time I meet a deadline. But a thank you would be nice sometimes. I know that's a weird request.

Mia: <u>It doesn't sound weird to me</u>. Let's figure this out!

What did you notice in this Do-Over? While it gets all the same information across as the original conversation, it also manages to send another message – not just how Mia thinks of the situation but also how Mia feels about Olivia as a person. As human beings, we are constantly processing information on these two levels:

1. What does the message mean?
2. How does this person feel about me?

Every interaction you have, whether with a coworker, a family member, or a stranger, sends these two sets of messages, intentionally or unintentionally. You may as well make it intentional.

Practice Station

One helpful way to visualize the dual-processing tendency is to picture this:

1. Information about the situation flowing over one shoulder.
2. Signals about how you feel about the person flowing over your other shoulder.

These two sides of the conversation are always present, even when you don't acknowledge them.

For example, in the midst of a disagreement with your manager, you might be consciously (or unconsciously) asking the following questions:

SITUATION		PERSON
Do you understand what happened? Do you have the information you need? Am I making myself clear?		Do you see me? Do you want to hear from me? Do you respect me? Do you care about me and want what's best for me?

Practice noticing these two "shoulders." Think about the last time you felt hurt. What happened over the "situation shoulder"? What message did you pick up over the "person shoulder"?

 Because people's brains are constantly pulling for both types of information, you must be just as deliberate about your "person messages" as you are about your "situation messages." This is where the **Validation** BU comes in. A **Validation** is essentially an answer to the (usually unspoken) questions hovering over the "person shoulder." Here are a few examples:

Validation Types	
Care statement:	*Example: I want to find a solution you're happy about.*
Normalizing statement:	*Example: Your reaction makes sense.*

Validation Types	
Acknowledgment:	*Example: This stuff is hard.*
Thanks:	*Example: Thank you for bringing this up to me.*

Three Reasons the Validation BU Helps You Become a Better Manager Faster

1. Validations Reduce Stress Faster

While some degree of stress can actually benefit performance, too much stress can quickly lead to mistakes, lost productivity, and even 45% less creativity (Grantcharov et al. 2018; Colonial Life 2019; Amabile et al. 2002). Even low but chronic levels of stress, like a chilly relationship with your manager, can fray your nerves enough to result in poor performance and even poor health. When we observed great managers, we saw that when they peppered **Validations** throughout their conversations, they put people at ease faster.

2. Validations Build Trust Faster

What makes people perceive someone as trustworthy? Most people assume that credibility and reliability are key. While that's true, one of the factors most folks underestimate in building trust is a sense of personal care (Green and Howe 2011). In other words, we humans trust others faster when we believe they want what's best for us. What is the impact of trust? High-trust teams are significantly more likely to be high-performing (de Jong et al. 2016). They are up-front about their thoughts, concerns, and even their mistakes – resulting in faster learning and better outcomes. When we trust people, we are also more likely to take their feedback seriously, leading to even faster improvements (Van Gennip et al. 2010).

3. Validations Increase Employee Retention

Gallup has spent decades studying predictors of employee engagement and retention. Just as our research at LifeLabs Learning has shown us that not all manager skills are created

Practice Station

Come up with **Validation** statements of your own (care, normalizing, acknowledgment, thanks) in response to each of the following comments:

Comment	Validation
I'm nervous about the presentation.	*Example: Yeah, I get that it's a lot of pressure.*
It seems like my opinion doesn't count.	*Example: I can see why it feels that way. Your opinion really does matter to me.*
I hate to admit it, but I think I made a mistake.	*Example: Thank you for telling me.*

equal, the researchers at Gallup have found that there is a small number of engagement survey questions that predict whether employees will stay or leave their company. One of the best predictors is the answer to the question "Does your supervisor, or someone at work, seem to care about you as a person?" (Clifton and Harter 2019). Of course, there are many ways to drive up the score to this question, but one of the fastest ways to show care is to come out and say it. **Validation** statements let you do just that.

***

In summary: People process information in two ways: (1) What does the message mean? (2) How does this person feel about me? Make your care for others explicit by using **Validations** like "That makes sense," "I care about your perspective," and even "Thanks!"

If you feel some resistance to using **Validations**, that's normal (see that **Validation** in action?). Attempting to send messages over the "person shoulder" can seem inauthentic at first. Remember, though: you are sending these messages constantly, whether you mean to do it or not. **Validating** simply means being deliberate about tending to information that always finds itself into a conversation. If you're uncomfortable, start small (for example: "Thanks for telling me that," "I hear you," "I'm glad you came to me with this") and use language that feels genuine to you. The goal is to remove ambiguity by making the implicit care you have for people explicit. Oh, by the way, great job making it to the end of this chapter. Thank you for reading ;)

MY LAB REPORT	Today's Date:
My takeaways:	

I regularly Vali-date others:	1 2 3 4 5 6 7 8 9 10 (strongly disagree) (strongly agree)
Experiment idea bank:	▪ If someone feels worried, then I will share a care statement. ▪ If someone is insecure, then I will offer a normalizing statement. ▪ If someone brings up a difficult topic with me, then I will thank them.
One small experiment I'll try to increase my score by 1 point:	
Post-experiment Learning Extractions:	

Bonus: Want to take your manager skills to the next level? Check out the bonus Inclusion Stations at leaderlab.lifelabs-learning.com.

My Learning Tracker

4 out of 7 Core BUs collected. 0 of 8 Core Skills collected.

Q-step	Playback	Deblur	Validate			

5

Linkup

Before we get into the BU in this chapter, see if anything in this conversation seems familiar:

Version 1

Luca: Hey, Mia. I found a web designer who can improve our landing page. We can even make updates this month.

Mia: Oh, okay . . . I didn't realize you were looking for a designer.

Luca: I wasn't, but this person is affordable and has a strong portfolio.

Mia: But we weren't planning to update the website, right? I thought we agreed that the priority for this quarter would be better analytics.

Luca: Oh yeah, I don't think we should drop the data project. I just think the website can be a lot better, and we still have enough budget left over to make it happen.

Have you ever found yourself in one of these discussions? How do you balance fanning the flames of people's enthusiasm with a focus on the most important work? Unfortunately, average managers tend to mishandle these tricky situations. The most common reactions are either to shut down the idea ("Sorry, but the website is just not a priority") or give in to the request ("Err . . . sure, we can always use a better-looking website"). By contrast, when we observed how great managers handled these scenarios, another important BU emerged: **"Linkup."**

We'll delve deeper into this BU as we get into other chapters (particularly Chapter 12), but in short, the **Linkup** is the explicit connection of an action to its goal. Picture a triangle with your goal perched at the top, and **Linkup** to this goal whenever you make a request, delegate, or give feedback. If your team members come to you with a "what" without a "why," ask **Linkup** questions (like "What does that link up to?") to help them connect to the top of that triangle.

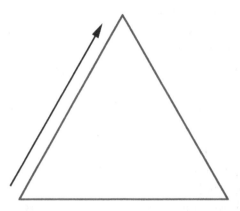

Source: LifeLabs Learning.

Reflecting on the conversation with Luca, Mia realizes that there was no clear "why" in the exchange. She was happy to see Luca's excitement, but she had no idea whether to approve the budget request. She decides to give it another go, so she hits the Do-Over Button:

Version 2: Do Over
Luca: Hey, Mia. I found a web designer who can improve our landing page. We can even make updates this month.
Mia: That's a helpful resource. Just so we're aligned: <u>what's your reasoning</u> for prioritizing the website this month?

Luca: Well, we haven't made any changes to it all year. It's starting to look dated.

Mia: Got it. And can you tell me more about your thinking: <u>what would you want to achieve</u> by improving the landing page?

Luca: Well . . . I'd want it to be more modern and better capture our brand.

Mia: Okay, so improved look and feel.

Luca: Yeah.

Mia: If the landing page looked more modern and on-brand, <u>what would the result be</u>?

Luca: I guess I'd want it to improve our conversion rates.

Mia: Sounds like you see our conversion rates as too low. Is that right?

Luca: Well, no. They're solid right now. But . . . they can always be better.

Mia: Yeah, agreed. So updating the website would be nice but not linked to our objectives?

Luca: Well, yeah. I guess it can wait given everything else we're working on.

Mia: That makes sense. <u>Was there any other reason</u> you were thinking of updating the website this month? <u>What else does it link up to</u>?

Luca: I mean, I just got excited about it. The analytics project is top priority, but honestly, it's kind of repetitive. Updating the website would be fun.

Mia: And I guess it would also be a new skill-building opportunity?

Luca: Yeah. You're right. But I also want to focus on something we actually need right now.

In this Do-Over, Mia's intention wasn't to demonstrate that updating the website isn't a good use of time. The result might have led to Mia discovering a new website is essential.

For example, in a parallel universe, the Do-Over Button might have led to the following conversation:

Version 3: Do-Over
Luca: Hey, Mia. I found a web designer who can improve our landing page. We can even make updates this month.
Mia: That's a helpful resource. Just so we're aligned: <u>what's your reasoning</u> for prioritizing the website this month?
Luca: Well, when I started working on the data analytics project, I realized that the setup of our website doesn't make it possible to track the data we need.
Mia: Oh! I didn't know that. <u>What would you be looking to achieve</u> with the changes?

Why the Linkup Is Such an Important Manager BU

1. Linkups Create Alignment Faster

 Without a clear and explicit **Linkup**, it can be easy to make progress toward different goals. For example, you might have three people on your team planning a conference. Without a **Linkup**, one person might be planning a conference that's as inexpensive as possible, another looking to drive the most attendance possible, and yet another hustling to bring in as much revenue as possible. While on the surface this sounds like the best conference ever (cheap, popular, and lucrative), in reality, this team will likely achieve small wins in several areas rather than a big win in the area that matters most. We hesitate to use the old "rowing in the same direction" analogy, but it's a good one when you consider the chaos that ensues when everyone is splashing in different directions. To create alignment faster, this team should discuss why they're planning a conference and how they'll measure success.

 A related payoff of **Linking up** is that it can shine a light on people's assumptions about the best way to achieve a result. Contrary to these authors' occasional power fantasies, when we say "jump" we do *not* want our team members asking "How high?" Instead, we want them asking "What are you looking to achieve by having us jump?" and even "What are some alternatives to jumping that might be better?" Perhaps a much better solution is to climb a ladder or even hire a jumping intern.

2. Linkups Enable Autonomy

Managers who only focus on the "what" without the "why" tend to become increasingly frustrated and wind up frustrating others. They answer dozens of "quick" questions about anything they assign, correcting (read: redoing) people's work, losing talented team members who get sick of being told what to do, and earning a reputation for being micromanagers. By contrast, managers who regularly **Linkup** give their team members autonomy to solve their own problems.

For example, if your team members know that the conference they're planning links up to increasing sales leads by 20% (while keeping conference costs below $100K), they can make decisions on their own without constantly checking in with you about everything from ticket costs to napkin colors. The **Linkup** becomes the ultimate guide for decision-making rather than the manager. What's the impact of greater autonomy? Increased speed and higher engagement.

3. Linkups Get You Buy-in Faster

 The **Linkup** BU also serves as fuel for increasing people's willingness to commit to your request faster. In a classic study by Ellen Langer and team (1978) – conducted back when copying machines were a thing in every college student's life – the research team shut down all copying machines in the university library except for one, in a devilish scheme to create a long queue. Next, a research assistant attempted to cut in line using one of three requests:

A. "Excuse me, I have 5 pages. May I use the Xerox machine?"
B. "Excuse me, I have 5 pages. May I use the Xerox machine because I have to make copies?"
C. "Excuse me, I have 5 pages. May I use the Xerox machine because I'm in a rush?"

Which of the conditions above would you expect to lead to better compliance? Check out the results below, showing the percentage of people who said yes:

A. 60%
B. 93%
C. 94%

Notice that even when the reasoning behind the request was weak (what else can you do with a copying machine except make copies?!), the "yes rate" skyrocketed. Making a request without a **Linkup** resulted in a compliance rate that is barely higher than a coin toss. Adding a simple "because" led to nearly perfect compliance. We aren't suggesting that you leverage these research findings by sharing vague **Linkups** ("Please plan a conference because I'd like us to have a conference") but because we want to remind you of the power of *because*. When people understand what's on top of that triangle, they make better decisions and are more motivated to take action.

Just as with other BUs we've shared with you so far, the **Linkup** comes in several flavors. Here are some examples:

Linkup Types	
Framing Linkup:	*The reason I ask is . . .* *My intention in doing this is . . .* *Can you help me understand your reasoning?*
Impact Linkup:	*The impact of doing this is . . .* *I mention it because . . .* *What do you see as the impact of this?*
Benefit Linkup:	*This will help us achieve . . .* *What's good about this is . . .* *What's important to you about it?*
Out-come Linkup:	*The end result should be . . .* *We're measuring success by . . .* *What's your definition of "done"?*
Passion Linkup:	*I'm really excited about this because . . .* *I love the idea of doing this since . . .* *What's most exciting to you about it?*
Overall Linkup:	*This links up to . . .* *What does this link up to?*

The only common **Linkup** question that doesn't consistently produce good results is "why?" There is something about that "why" question that tends to trigger defensiveness and signal judgment rather than authentic curiosity. Even hostage negotiators deliberately avoid why questions (Voss and Raz 2016). See if you can sense the difference between the original conversation, followed by Mia's quick Do-Over:

VERSION 1: WHY	VERSION 2: LINKUP DO-OVER
Olivia: I was thinking of inviting a few clients to join our planning committee. **Mia:** Why would you do that?	**Olivia:** I was thinking of inviting a few clients to join our planning committee. **Mia:** What do you hope to achieve?

Better yet, in Version 2, Mia could have also thrown in a **Validation**, especially if Olivia seemed hesitant to share the idea. Depending on the culture of the team and their level of confidence and trust, a "why" question might work just as well, but a different **Linkup** question is less likely to invite self-doubt and defensiveness.

Linking up can act as a "pull" mechanism, drawing out people's reasoning by asking **Linkup** questions. And of course, it can also serve a "push" function, giving people access to the "why" behind your messages. Let's sit in on Mia's first conversation with her new hire, Kofi. See how it goes when the **Linkup** is lost in their first conversation:

Version 1
Mia: Hi, Kofi. It's great to finally get to work together. **Kofi:** Thanks, I'm glad to be here. **Mia:** Wonderful. I set aside time for you to review training materials later today. I thought we could use this time to talk about our team. How does that sound?

> **Kofi:** Sounds great!
> **Mia:** Great! Well, let's start with the team. As you know, we gather, analyze, and present data for our clients. Do you have any questions about that?

This is not a bad onboarding conversation. But it's not great. Mia misses out on opportunities to give Kofi context, clarity, and motivation for the work. She can sense it almost as soon as the conversation gets going, so Mia hits the Do-Over Button and tries again:

***

Version 2: Do-Over

Mia: Hi, Kofi. It's great to finally get to work together.
Kofi: Thanks, I'm glad to be here.
Mia: Wonderful. I set aside time for you to review training materials later today <u>so you can</u> already start to become familiar with our systems. I thought we could use this time to talk about our team <u>because</u> I want to give you visibility into why we do what we do. <u>The benefit</u> of starting this way is the rest of the training will make more sense. How does that sound?
Kofi: Sounds great!
Mia: Great! Well, let's start with the team. As you know, we gather, analyze, and present data for our clients. <u>The reason our work matters</u> is that we help our cli-

ents make great decisions. Without us, everyone would just be taking guesses. <u>I personally love what we do because</u> we help people feel more secure and confident every day. How about you? <u>What's exciting for you</u> about doing this work?

Practice Station

Your turn! Get some practice **Linking up** your work to why it matters. For each prompt below, figure out your **Linkup**:

Item	Linkup
For an item on your to-do list:	*Example: Getting this done will achieve . . .*
For a recent decision you made:	*Example: This was the right decision because . . .*
For a goal your team is trying to achieve:	*Example: This goal is important because . . .*
For your work as a manager:	*Example: My work matters because . . .*

In summary: Link up to a *why* whenever you make a request, set a goal, delegate, or give feedback. Ask **Linkup** questions whenever the link is unclear. For example: "What does this link up to?" Not only do great managers share **Linkups** and ask **Linkup** questions of others, but we were surprised to see that these managers often asked **Linkup** questions of themselves. For example, several managers we interviewed had the habit of asking, "Why am I doing this right now?" At times, our behavior can be just as puzzling to us as other people's actions. **Linking up** helps us reorient and make the best use of our time. Speaking of which, what's your **Linkup** for reading this book?

MY LAB REPORT	Today's Date:
My takeaways:	
I regularly share and ask for Linkups:	1 2 3 4 5 6 7 8 9 10 (strongly disagree) (strongly agree)
Experiment idea bank:	• If I delegate, then I'll Link up to the goal. • If I give feedback, then I'll share the impact. • If someone makes a suggestion, then I'll ask a Linkup question.
One small experiment I'll try to increase my score by 1 point:	
Post-experiment Learning Extractions:	

Bonus: Want to take your manager skills to the next level? Check out the bonus Inclusion Stations at leaderlab.lifelabs-learning.com.

My Learning Tracker

5 out of 7 Core BUs collected. 0 of 8 Core Skills collected.

Q-step	Playback	Deblur	Validate	LinkUp		

6

Pause

You've now learned most of the core BUs you'll need to include in your very own Swiss Army knife of manager excellence. That's a lot of cognitive work. So let's take a quick break before we move onto the next BU.

Practice Station

Try an exercise (from the Benson-Henry Institute for Mind Body Medicine) that's popular among a wide range of professions, from yogis to Navy Seals. Starting with the lower left-hand corner of the rectangle in the image, use one finger to trace the left, vertical line up to the left-hand corner, while slowly inhaling and counting to five. Next, trace your finger from the upper left-hand corner to the upper right-hand corner, while slowly exhaling and counting to seven. Then, inhale slowly while tracing down the right side for five counts. And exhale slowly while tracing across to the left side for seven counts. Make your way around three times.

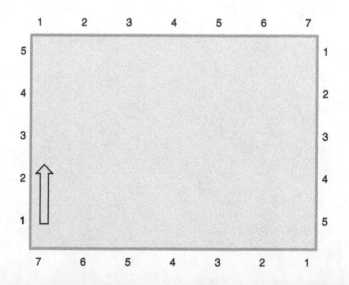

How was that? While this exercise takes about one minute to complete, most people report feeling significantly refreshed and relaxed. This is the surprising finding we came across in our manager research at LifeLabs Learning: the most productive managers take the time to do . . . nothing. As lifelong workaholics ourselves, we (the authors) were skeptical about this finding. But there it was again and again. Doing nothing is often the best thing to do. And doing nothing well is a skill. We refer to this deceptively active BU as "**Pause.**" Despite the overwhelming pressure most of us carry to do more and do it faster, taking time to **Pause** yields better results.

Let's Pause and Talk About Why Pausing Is So Important for Managers

1. Pausing Creates Sustained Productivity

A delightful paradox of productivity is that people often achieve more when they take the time to do less. It turns out that brains (and bodies) tend to work best in bursts – varying from intense focus to complete rest (Trougakos and Hideg 2009). We refer to this ability to skillfully swing from expanding to recapturing energy as "oscillation competence." Great managers are great oscillators and help develop oscillation competence in others too.

2. Pausing Sparks Innovation Faster

Where would our understanding of science be today if an apple hadn't fallen on Sir Isaac Newton's head? Did the apple knock the idea of gravity into Newton's mind that day? Not exactly. The insight appeared because Newton spent many hours working on the concept, and then . . . **Paused.** Perhaps you haven't made a discovery similar to the magnitude of gravity (yet), but you have likely also had your best ideas pop up at odd times – like those classic mid-shower aha moments. In fact, whenever you are stuck on a problem, have an important decision to make, or want to push yourself and your team to produce innovative thinking faster, intense focus followed by **Pause** is the best strategy. For even more impressive results, include movement into your **Pause** time. Research shows that walking while thinking increases creative output by 60% (Oppezzo and Schwartz 2014).

3. Pausing Resolves Conflict Faster

Perhaps the greatest rewards of **Pausing** are evident in times of conflict. When your stress levels rise, your heart rate accelerates, and your peripheral vision actually narrows – making your attention narrow as well (Williams, Tonymon, and Andersen 1990). This trifecta forces you to focus only on the task in front of you, which can get you stuck on the mental equivalent of the gas pedal. Add anger to the mix, and your need for speed intensifies. More **Pause** leads to clearer thinking, which leads to less destructive conflict and faster resolution.

Psychologist John Gottman found that, much like in the workplace, **Pausing** is also one of the best predictors of successful marriages. Gottman is famous for predicting with 93.6% accuracy which couples will stay together and which will break up. He has joked that this skillset makes him an unpopular dinner party guest. That said, it has made him an extraordinarily successful researcher. By studying thousands of hours of couples' interactions, Gottman identified that **Pausing** just at the point of conflict escalation was one of the single best predictors of relationship longevity (Gottman 1999). These skillful couples either **Paused** and de-escalated (apologized, made a joke, spoke more softly) or they called a total timeout.

Take a look at the following conversion, and determine where Mia could have **Paused** to help the situation. Hint: notice where the conversation escalates and insert the **Pause** there.

Version 1

Luca: I can't believe you left me out of another meeting! I thought we talked about this.

Mia: Oh! I didn't even know you wanted to be there.

Luca: Why wouldn't I want to be there? It was my idea in the first place.

Mia: What? How could you say it was your idea? This entire thing only happened because I suggested it.

Luca: I can't believe you're taking all the credit for this. Do you know how hard I worked to make this possible? I even had to miss my mother's birthday just to make the deadline!

Mia: Well, no one asked you to miss your mother's birthday, Luca.

Ouch. There were several opportunities to rescue this conversation, but one moment in particular was begging for a **Pause**. Did you spot it? Once Mia is able to calm down from this exchange, she wishes she had a magical Pause Button handy too. But since her only time-controlling device is the Do-Over Button, she decides to hit the button and try the conversation again:

Version 2: Do-Over

Luca: I can't believe you left me out of yet another meeting! I thought we talked about this.

Mia: Oh! I didn't even know you wanted to be there.

Luca: Why wouldn't I want to be there? It was my idea in the first place.

Mia: *[Pause]*

Luca: I mean . . . I know we all made it happen together, but I was really proud of it.

Mia: I hear you. It sounds like you felt left out at the most important part.

Luca: Yeah.

Mia: *[Pause]*

Luca: I even missed my mom's birthday because I was trying to meet the deadline.

Mia: *[Pause]*

Luca: I know that's not your fault. It was my choice. But I was really looking forward to that meeting and seeing everyone's reaction to the analytics dashboard now that it's all done.

Mia: Of course. I'm sorry I didn't include you. It's important to me that you get to see the payoff of your work. I know it might be too late, but what's something I might be able to do now or maybe in the future to make sure you're included?

Luca: Thanks. I know you didn't mean to leave me out. Sorry I got so heated. Would it be possible to get the notes from the meeting and join the next one?

There are three types of **Pauses** the managers we interviewed reported taking regularly, with category names inspired by psychologist Tal Ben-Shahar:

Micro Pauses *(a few seconds or minutes)*	**Examples:** • Pause to **Q-step** before answering a question. • Pause to breathe before responding when hurt or angry. • Pause to **Linkup** before starting a new task or project. • Pause to stretch, get up, or take a mini-dance break.
Meso Pauses *(one or more hours)*	**Examples:** • Pause to exercise. • Pause to eat an uninterrupted meal. • Pause to move away from a challenge when stuck. • Pause to reflect on the week's goals.
Macro Pauses *(one or more days)*	**Examples:** • Pause for a full day to **Extract** learnings from the year. • Pause for several days to do long-term planning. • Pause to "unplug" pre- or post-work and on the weekends. • Pause to take a full-blown vacation.

Pausing does not come naturally to people. We humans aren't wired for it. In fact, when people are threatened, our brains' amygdalae can even go so far as to reroute how we process information. Instead of sending data to your neocortex (the area of the brain responsible for rational thought), the triggered amygdalae activate the limbic system. This response can be so extreme that psychologists refer to it as "amygdala hijacking" – a term popularized by emotion researcher Daniel Goleman (2005). The amygdalae "hijack" people's minds, making them operate in fight-or-flight mode before they fully realize what's happening. In practice, this looks like sweaty palms, a racing heart, and a one-way ticket to Regretsville after certain words fly out of your mouth or off your fingertips. It was a helpful adaptation for our ancestors who used it to react swiftly to saber-toothed tigers. It is a pesky neural system when it kicks in at work.

So, on the one hand, **Pausing** is nearly impossible once we are "hijacked." And on the other hand, it is the only way to regain cortical control. How do you navigate the paradox of needing a **Pause** just when **Pausing** is most difficult? Gottman found that the most successful couples had a timeout cue (like shouting "avocado!") to sharply break up a fight. The taxi drivers we mentioned in Chapter 1 learned to **Pause** by labeling their "honk urge." The managers we studied also shared a variety of **Pausing** if-thens that worked for them. For example:

> "If I start to hear ringing in my ears and my neck tenses up, I know it's time for me to take a break. Even if I'm in the middle of a sentence, I'll excuse myself and go wash my face to cool off."
>
> "The other person's voice is a good reminder to just slow everything down. If they start raising their voice, that's my cue to shut up. If they calm down, great. If not, I just say, 'I'm having a tough time thinking clearly. Can we come back to this tomorrow?'"
>
> "If I notice myself getting defensive, before I say anything I just silently count backwards from 10. Usually, that's enough time for me to think of something better to say."

To become a great manager faster, start planning your **Pauses** in advance. Following are some of our favorite examples from the leaders we studied:

Sample Pauses

- Pause every morning to decide on your top thing to accomplish that day.
- Designate a "big picture thinking" time and place. (One executive we studied told us she even had a special thinking chair; another senior leader sat at his desk just thinking for an hour every day to model the importance of taking thinking time.)
- Take a social break every day and use it as a chance to meet a new coworker.
- Treat your weekends as vacation days: put all work away and do something that you find reenergizing.

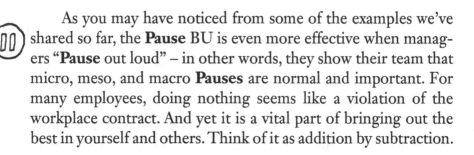

As you may have noticed from some of the examples we've shared so far, the **Pause** BU is even more effective when managers "**Pause** out loud" – in other words, they show their team that micro, meso, and macro **Pauses** are normal and important. For many employees, doing nothing seems like a violation of the workplace contract. And yet it is a vital part of bringing out the best in yourself and others. Think of it as addition by subtraction.

Practice Station

Plan out your **Pauses** in advance. Write down one **Pause** ritual idea for each **Pause** type:

Micro Pauses (a few seconds or minutes):

Meso Pauses (one or more hours):

Macro Pauses (one or more days):

***

In summary: Take micro, meso, and macro **Pauses** to increase productivity and creativity, and to reduce unproductive conflict. **Pause** out loud to normalize and encourage your team to **Pause** too. To practice this BU right away, take a short **Pause** before you move onto the next chapter.

MY LAB REPORT	Today's Date:
My takeaways:	

I regularly take the time to Pause:	1 2 3 4 5 6 7 8 9 10 (strongly disagree) (strongly agree)
Experiment idea bank:	▪ If it's the start of my day, then I will Pause to create a plan. ▪ If I've been sitting for an hour, then I will stretch and take a deep breath. ▪ If I notice someone is upset, I will Pause and listen rather than speak.
One small experiment I'll try to increase my score by 1 point:	
Post-experiment Learning Extractions:	

Bonus: Want to take your manager skills to the next level? Check out the bonus Inclusion Stations at leaderlab.lifelabs-learning.com.

My Learning Tracker

6 out of 7 Core BUs collected. 0 of 8 Core Skills collected.

Q-step	Playback	Deblur	Validate	Linkup	Pause		

7

Extract

The following is a short excerpt from a debrief between two fighter pilots (Lemoine 2019). Technical jargon aside, see if you notice what makes this conversation special:

Lemoine: A couple of things I need to clean up – I could have been a little bit more clear on, kind of, the setups and what I was looking for and how we were gonna run that . . . . Did you have any questions from the brief? Anything that came up in the air that, you know, you're like hey, I could have maybe briefed that a little bit better?

Wags: Nah, negative.

Lemoine: So departure . . . the only thing I had was on the rejoin for the initial takeoff. If you would have just cut to the inside that probably would have saved us a little bit of gas. But otherwise, I thought the rejoin was expeditious.

The debrief continues in this way for 24 minutes and 30 seconds. They review every moment of the short flight point by point from brief to takeoff to landing. Their tone throughout is calm and matter-of-fact. What makes this debrief special? Nothing, actually. Commenting on the debrief, Lemoine says:

> *"This is just how a debrief works. Wags did a great job, but we debrief. No one has a perfect flight. No one does everything perfect because if they did, we would never have to train. So, we train. We make mistakes. We learn. We debrief, and we do better."*

In the world of aviation, debriefs are a mandatory wrap-up to every flight. In the world of leadership, not so much. And yet we found that the great managers we studied acted a lot like seasoned pilots. Rather than solving a challenge, forgetting it, and moving on, they **Pause** and mine the experience for new learning. We call this BU "**Extract**."

To visualize how **Extracting** works, let's briefly turn our leader lab into a chemistry lab. Chemical extraction is a separation process, isolating one substance from a matrix of components. Without extraction, we'd never have tea from leaves, vanilla extract from beans, or vodka from potatoes.

In the same way, there are "molecules" of insight floating around every experience we have. These rich lessons can be invisible on the surface. In fact, many of them can even look like moments of failure and frustration, experiences we'd much rather forget than turn to for personal development. But when you deliberately **Extract** the learning, you can uncover countless lessons just waiting to be learned.

Of all the BUs we teach managers in our workshops at LifeLabs Learning, this one gets the most raised eyebrows. Most people assume that learning happens when we find out about new concepts or apply the concepts firsthand. These forms of learning are all important, but a little-known truth about the brain is that people learn best when they reflect. In fact, reflecting can even lead to more rapid skill-building than additional practice (Karpicke 2012). According to the famous education reformer John Dewey, reflection should include a look back at actions *and* emotions and ideally done together with others (Rodgers 2002).

Many of the great managers we studied had an "after-action review" template of some kind for themselves and their teams. Many call it a retro or a debrief and several use the term "blameless post-mortem" (the key word being "blameless" to keep the focus on the situation rather than the person). Whatever the name, the most common components include:

1. What went well
2. What didn't go well
3. What we can do differently next time

Most managers admit that the first few team reviews are typically uncomfortable. The mood is tense and everyone is coiled tight and ready to spring with justifications for their actions. Once the ritual becomes familiar and team members realize that the focus is on learning, they relax into the process and start to enjoy it. The more predictable the cadence (for instance: after every project, at the end of every sprint, on the first Monday of every month), the more fluent the team becomes in **Extracting** the learning together and the more quickly they improve.

Aside from **Extracting** the learning as a team, several managers we interviewed mentioned that they encourage each team member to **Extract** individual learnings. Here are two examples:

> *"I like to make a big deal when something goes right. I try to shine a big flashlight on it and ask, 'Hey, that was great what you did there! What made you do that? What was going through your mind? How are you going to remember to do it next time?'"*
>
> *"We do a 'year in review' on people's anniversaries. It's a really nice tradition. You look back on the year and write down your accomplishments, lessons learned, relationships built. Sometimes, you don't realize how far you've come and how much you've changed until you look back at that starting line."*

Just about any conversation can be an opportunity to **Extract** the learning. Take a look at the following exchange and spot the **Extraction** opportunities Mia misses:

Version 1
Mia: Hey, Kofi. How did your first week go?
Kofi: Overall, I think it was okay! Better than I expected.
Mia: Oh, that's great to hear. Congrats!
Kofi: Yeah. It's a relief to get through my first week. There were a few things I could have done better, but I'm trying not to beat myself up about it.
Mia: Good. You've put in a lot of effort. You should be proud of yourself.

Again, Mia didn't do a *bad* job. This conversation was supportive and encouraging. Alas, it also allowed a learning opportunity to slip by. What would you have done differently to **Extract** the learning? Let's look at the Do-Over Mia decides to try:

Version 2: Do-Over

Mia: Hey, Kofi. How did your first week go?

Kofi: Overall, I think it was okay! Better than I expected.

Mia: Oh, great! <u>What was better than expected?</u>

Kofi: I was honestly worried about forgetting everything as soon as I learned it, but the information actually stuck.

Mia: Terrific. There's so much more to remember, so it would be great to extract the learning. <u>What do you think helped make the information stick?</u>

Kofi: Well, first I was trying to memorize everything on the spot. But it was stressing me out, so what worked well was writing down the key points from every training session on a separate page in my notebook, then reviewing my notes at the end of every day.

Mia: That's such a good insight to apply in the coming weeks. <u>Is there any other learning you want to extract from what went well or what could have been better?</u>

 Aside from helping others learn, perhaps most admirable of all is that great managers are constantly **Extracting** their own learning. Any time they do something new or collaborate with someone new, they **Pause** to **Extract**. They also **Extract** insights from others by "pulling" for feedback. In other words, they ask for feedback rather than waiting until someone decides to "push" it to them (stay tuned for more on how to do this well in Chapter 9).

Every day that passes can become an education for the day that follows. The more skilled the managers we studied were, the hungrier they seemed to be for feedback and the more willing they were to learn. Although this correlation between experience and humility surprised us, it turns out to be a fairly common phenomenon, dubbed the Dunning-Kruger effect (Kruger and Dunning 1999).

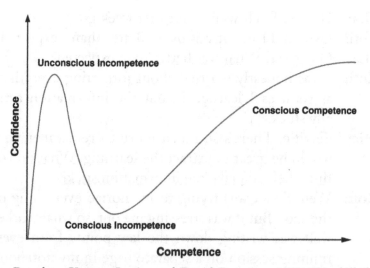

Source: Based on Kruger, Justin, and David Dunning. 1999. "Unskilled and Unaware of It: How Difficulties in Recognizing One's Own Incompetence Lead to Inflated Self-Assessments." Journal of Personality and Social Psychology, 77, no. 6: 1121–1134.

Though the Dunning-Kruger effect has been challenged by some researchers, it rang true in our experience. The most confident and least curious managers we studied were usually also the least competent – a state known as "unconscious incompetence." The more quickly people recognize the gap between their current skill level and their desired skill level, the more rapidly they're able to close that gap. Best of all, the more a leader models this learning mindset, the more likely it is to permeate throughout the team culture, resulting in faster learning, better results, and fewer coworkers trapped in that annoying overconfidence that comes from unconscious incompetence.

 Following are several distinct **Extraction** varieties we've come across in our research:

Extraction Types	
Reflect and apply	Ask yourself and others what you can learn from an experience and how you can apply the lessons learned in the future. *Example: I want to make sure we're getting the most out of this experience. What would you say your biggest learnings were? How can we apply these in the future?*
Pull for feedback	Ask what you did well and not so well. *Example: So that I can keep learning, would you share what you thought went well and what could be better, even if it's just a 10% improvement?*
Demarcate	Give a <u>label</u> to a learning moment to make it more tangible. *Example: I noticed that interaction you had with the customer. Nice job using your <u>influence skills</u>. What did you learn from that exchange?*
Do a pre-mortem *A practice introduced by psychologist Gary Klein (2007)*	Before a project begins, assume it will be an epic failure. Work backwards to determine the cause of the failure and generate ideas to prevent it. *Example: Let's imagine this is a total flop. What could lead to the initiative failing? What can we do now to avoid those issues?*

Practice Station

Take a moment now to choose an **Extraction** cue for yourself. For example, every time you get into the elevator at work, ask, "What did I learn today?"

This final Core BU is actually the most important one you can add to your manager toolkit. **Extracting** is like an accelerant for every other BU. Want to master all seven Core BUs 20 times faster than it would take you to learn through experience alone? After every one-on-one and meeting you have, ask the **Extraction** questions below. Within seven weeks, your brain will have a learning **Extraction** habit. This superpower is like having your very own Do-Over Button!

Practice Station

Set a reminder on your phone or calendar now to ask these **Extraction** questions:

Week 1: Q-step	When did I tell instead of asking? What can I repeat or do differently next time?

Week 2: Playback	How effectively did I Play back what I heard? What can I repeat or do differently next time?
Week 3: Deblur	What blur words did I catch and Deblur? What can I repeat or do differently next time?
Week 4: Validate	How effectively did I Validate people in the conversation? What can I repeat or do differently next time?
Week 5: Linkup	How clear were the Linkups for everyone involved? What can I repeat or do differently next time?
Week 6: Pause	When did I rush where a Pause could have helped? What can I repeat or do differently next time?
Week 7: Extract	How effectively did I Extract the learning? What can I repeat or do differently next time?

***

In summary: Get more out of every experience by **Extracting** the learning and helping others do it too. Reflect on what worked well or could be better, pull for feedback, and demarcate learning. In retrospect, it's not odd that **Extracting** is one of the BUs that distinguish great managers from the average folks. Managers who regularly **Extract** just keep getting better faster. And look! It's time for your final BU Lab Report. If you've been completing these reports thus far, you've been **Extracting** all along. Well done, you. What do you want to **Extract** from this chapter?

MY LAB REPORT	Today's Date:
My takeaways:	
I regularly Extract learnings:	1 2 3 4 5 6 7 8 9 10 (strongly disagree) (strongly agree)
Experiment idea bank:	• If I've had a tough conversation, then I will Extract the learning. • If someone does something well, then I will ask them how they did it. • If my team has completed a project, then I will schedule a retrospective.
One small experiment I'll try to increase my score by 1 point:	
Post-experiment Learning Extractions:	

Bonus: Want to take your manager skills to the next level? Check out the bonus Inclusion Stations at leaderlab.lifelabs-learning.com.

My Learning Tracker

7 out of 7 Core BUs collected. 0 of 8 Core Skills collected.

Q-step	Playback	Deblur	Validate	Linkup	Pause	Extract

The Core Skills

Congratulations! You have now collected all seven Core BUs – the small Behavioral Units that came up again and again in our research at LifeLabs Learning as the distinguishing behaviors of great managers. These BUs alone will make you a better manager faster by helping you create clarity, drive alignment, build trust, mitigate bias, and accelerate learning. But to become a truly great manager – someone who catalyzes engagement and helps people achieve amazing results – you need to know how to wield your leadership Swiss Army knife in an infinite array of situations. You'll need to mix and match different BUs to develop leadership *skills*.

What's the difference between a BU and a skill? As an analogy, consider the importance of strengthening your physical core muscles. Think of a strong physical core as a BU. While this BU alone is great to have, its true power comes from what it makes possible. With a strong core, you can more quickly develop your athleticism, posture, flexibility, and many other skills. Skills are more complex and take longer to master than BUs, but they will let you tackle an even greater array of obstacles and opportunities as a leader. The Core BUs you've learned so far are at the foundation of most leadership skills and will help you develop these skills faster.

Which leadership skills matter most? While the great managers we studied displayed dozens of skills, we found that a small set of just eight *Core Skills* came up more than any others across a wide range of leadership scenarios (from handling tough conversations to keeping people focused in times of uncertainty). Because mastering these Core Skills opens the door to countless other competencies faster, we refer to them as "tipping point skills." These are the smallest changes that make the biggest impact in the shortest time. These skills are:

1. Coaching Skills
2. Feedback Skills

3. Productivity Skills
4. Effective One-on-Ones
5. Strategic Thinking
6. Meetings Mastery
7. Leading Change
8. People Development

Before you move on to this next floor of the leader lab, take five minutes to complete this self-assessment, based on the Core Skills you're about to learn. This exercise will help you learn more quickly and track your progress along the way:

Leadership Scenarios Self-Assessment	Score 1–10 (10 = highest)
1. Imagine you have a team member who is demotivated by their work. *How confident are you that you know how to coach them to find more motivation?*	
2. Let's say someone on your team comes across as dismissive when others share ideas. *How confident are you that you know how to give them feedback?*	
3. Assume that one of your team members is constantly overwhelmed, falling behind on deadlines, and having trouble focusing. *How confident are you that you know how to help?*	
4. Effective one-on-one meetings increase engagement, development, and productivity. *How confident are you that you know how to achieve these results with the one-on-ones you have with each person on your team?*	

Leadership Scenarios Self-Assessment	Score 1–10 (10 = highest)
5. Imagine that your team is working on a large, complex, cross-functional project. *How confident are you that you know how to help them think strategically and avoid common strategic thinking mistakes?*	
6. Let's say you are leading a meeting where some people are going off topic, some are overtalking, and it's unclear how the group should make a decision. *How confident are you that you know how to course-correct and get the meeting back on track?*	
7. When change happens, team members often resist it or avoid it. *How confident are you that you know how to gain buy-in?*	
8. Assume that one of your team members feels like they are not learning and growing. *How confident are you that you know how to help them develop in ways that are meaningful to them and helpful for the company?*	
9. Great managers know how to leverage their team's diversity, mitigate bias, and make each person feel valued and respected. *How confident are you that you know how to be inclusive?*	
10. Great leaders are also great learners. *How confident are you that you know how to keep learning and growing as a manager?*	
Total leadership confidence score:	

Now that you've taken some time to reflect, let's move on to collect those new skills.

8

Coaching Skills

When we asked our clients to let us study their best managers (in terms of their ability to catalyze engagement and performance), the number one skill that stood out among these masterful managers is *coaching*. In fact, coaching skills are the very foundation of great leadership. This multifaceted tipping point skill also spills over into countless domains, including every skill we'll present in this book and many others (like influence, negotiation, persuasion, and conflict resolution). To become a great manager faster, focus on becoming a great coach faster.

What Coaching Is (and Isn't)

Let's begin by **Deblurring** what coaching is. Many of us hear the word "coach" and conjure images of sports coaches shouting from the sidelines, eyes bulging, and spit flying. But coaching in the modern workplace is different. There are fewer statements, more questions, and (usually) less spit. In short, *coaching is the process of helping people develop capacity to achieve results.*

Unlike directing or advising, coaching is all about catalyzing insights *within* others. As a visual representation of the difference between directing and coaching (which is also a key difference between average and great managers), imagine two boxing trainers watching their fighters in the ring. One trainer is shouting and gesticulating wildly. The other trainer is sitting back and observing in silence. The loud trainer yells, "Hey, that's bad leadership! Why aren't you telling your fighter what to do?" Just as the loud trainer's fighter gets knocked out, the quiet trainer replies, "I'm not the one in the ring. I train my fighters to solve their own problems."

How can you tell if developing your coaching skills will help you and your team win more proverbial matches? Here are several common symptoms of leaning too heavily on directing and not enough on coaching. See if you can recognize yourself in any of them:

- You are trapped in a hamster wheel of "quick questions" from your team members that you must answer so they can make progress.
- Your team members don't take initiative, propose ideas, or make decisions without you.
- You avoid delegating because you don't trust work will get done well, and when you do delegate, you end up redoing people's work.

The 4Cs: Noticing Coaching Moments Faster

If any of these symptoms ring a bell, coaching is likely to be your antidote. One of the fastest ways to develop your coaching skills is to get good at noticing when you have a coaching opportunity. How do you know when it's time to coach? Here are the four most common flags. We call them the *4Cs*:

1. **Conundrum:** Someone asks you how to handle their conundrum (like a problem or decision) and either has the capacity to solve it on their own or can build skills or confidence by doing it.
2. **Complaint:** Someone complains to you about a person, a situation, or a conflict.
3. **Confidence:** Someone is indecisive or insecure, so they are asking you to make a decision or take action instead of doing it themselves.
4. **Completion:** Someone has completed a project or reached a goal.

While most people see these *4C* situations as problems or frustrations, great managers recognize that they are actually openings to rapidly scale their team's capacity to do great work. Developing strong coaching skills takes years, but you can accelerate your coaching prowess by honing two leadership habits: (1) using a coaching framework we call the "*SOON Funnel*" and (2) continuously honing your **Q-step** BU. These are the two coaching competencies we'll focus on throughout the rest of this chapter.

The Coaching SOON Funnel

Since coaching is all about helping people **Extract** insights based on what they already know, one of the easiest ways to become a better coach faster is to ask more questions. But it's not just question *quantity* that counts. Question *quality* is also essential. A simple way to ask higher-quality coaching questions is to use a coaching framework. The framework we've developed at LifeLabs Learning based on our observations of great managers is called the *SOON Funnel*. **SOON** stands for **S**uccess, **O**bstacles, **O**ptions, and **N**ext Steps.

Playbacks + Split-tracks

Success: What does success look like?

Obstacles: What are the obstacles?

Options: What are the options?

Next Steps: What are the next steps?

We refer to *SOON* as a funnel because the focus narrows with each level of coaching questions. Instead of asking questions that take people in a wide range of directions, the *SOON Funnel* creates an efficient conversational "shape" that drives toward a resolution *soon*er. To ensure clarity and help people feel heard, you can also pepper in **Playbacks** throughout (the BU we first introduced in Chapter 2).

Let's join Mia again as she attempts to coach Olivia. This is a Conundrum and a Complaint – a definite coaching moment. As you observe the conversation, consider what Mia does well and what she could do even better:

Version 1

Olivia: You know Jeff, the finance team manager? Working with him is a nightmare. Every time I come to him with an issue, he makes it sound like it's *our* fault. I don't even have enough time to fix our issues, let alone his.

Mia: Sounds like two things – the issue with Jeff and the time issue. Which of those should we tackle first?

Olivia: Jeff, for sure.

Mia: Okay, got it. So, what do you think is causing the problem?

Olivia: Him! His attitude, honestly.

Mia: What's something you haven't tried yet that might work?

Olivia: I guess I can be sterner, like he is. Or maybe I can have someone else be his main point of contact instead?

Mia: Who are you considering?

Olivia: Well, Kofi is too new. And you're too busy. Luca could be good since he's pretty direct. Maybe that style would work better?

Mia: I can see that. How would you make the transition to Luca?

> **Olivia:** I don't know. I'm not sure if it's the right way to go because it seems unfair. Like if I can't deal with it, why make it someone else's problem? I could just give Jeff feedback.
>
> **Mia:** Feedback is great.
>
> **Olivia:** Ugh. I don't know. I don't think he would take it well.

This was a good coaching conversation, but it wasn't great. Though Mia asked many questions, did **Playbacks**, **Deblurred**, and **Validated**, it didn't result in a solution. Sometimes that's okay. Many problems are too hefty to solve right away. But Mia missed some opportunities to solve it sooner. So let's briefly look at each level of the *SOON Funnel* one by one so you can end this chapter ready to put this tool to use (and Mia can give her conversation another go).

SOON Funnel: "Success" Coaching Questions

Most people talk about their problems by focusing on what's going wrong, but thinking about possibilities sparks more creativity than focusing on challenges. Not only does starting coaching conversations with Success questions put people in a more productive state of mind, but it also helps them **Linkup** to what they're actually trying to achieve. A simple definition of a problem is: *success + obstacles*. Until you **Pause** to name what success means to you, it becomes nearly impossible to generate ideas for helpful solutions.

Sample Success Questions

- What does success look like to you?
- What's important to you about that?
- What do you hope to achieve?
- What would tell you you've reached your goal?
- What is your definition of "done"?

SOON Funnel: "Obstacles" Coaching Questions

Once the definition of success is **Deblurred**, it's time to complete the problem statement (*success + obstacles*). The gap between success and obstacles is the crux of any problem. While it might be tempting to leap into generating solutions, great managers model the discipline to identify the actual problem first. Skip this level, and you will either end up with a solution to the wrong problem or you'll be trapped in a conversation where every option is met with a "Yeah, but." If the person you're coaching is hesitant to talk about their problems, be sure to **Validate** their efforts by thanking them for sharing or acknowledging that the challenge is difficult.

Sample Obstacles Questions

- What are the obstacles?
- What concerns you most about it?
- What is standing in the way of achieving your goal?
- Who might be negatively impacted?
- What might be some unintended consequences?

SOON Funnel: "Options" Coaching Questions

Here comes the fun part! This is the level of the funnel most managers enjoy because it's where the solving happens most visibly. If you've done a good job defining the problem (*success* + *obstacles*), this part of the coaching conversation will be surprisingly easy. That said, we still encourage exploring multiple options even if the first idea that comes to mind sounds promising. Research shows that generating more options leads to better outcomes (Nutt 2004). The Options level works best when you **Extract** and consider all ideas, even/especially the oddballs. If you are eager to throw in your own suggestions, this is a good place to do it; just **Pause** and resist that temptation to offer advice until you've given the other person time to come up with their own ideas.

Sample Options Questions

- What are your options? (What else?)
- What have you tried so far?
- If you could do anything, what would you do?
- What's different about times this problem isn't there? (What ideas does that give you?)
- Who else has solved a similar problem?

SOON Funnel: "Next Steps" Coaching Questions

Once there are multiple viable options, move the coaching conversation to a space of action and accountability. With simple problems, you'll likely be able to get to "Next steps" within one conversation. With complex problems or when working with people who need more processing or solo-thinking time, you can create Pause by saying, "How about you think through different ideas, then we can discuss them next week and decide on next steps?" For important actions or decisions, get the next steps in writing in a shared document. Writing helps Deblur the plan. What's more, when people write down their goals, they achieve them at a rate of 76%, rather than 36% for unwritten goals (Matthews 2015).

Sample Next Steps Questions

- What are your next steps?
- What is the first small step? (What's an even smaller step you can take?)
- What is your plan?
- When will you start?
- When should we check in about it again?

Practice Station

Want an easy way to remember the *SOON Funnel*? Our memories are strengthened when we have a kinesthetic anchor (Casasanto and de Bruin 2019). **Try this:**

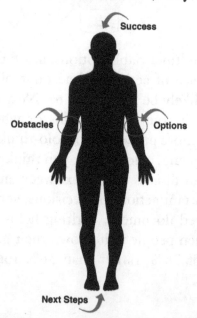

Remember *SOON* by associating each letter with a part of your body.

- Touch your forehead to remember to start with **S**uccess questions because it's where you visualize success.
- Touch your left elbow to ask **O**bstacles questions – since bent elbow tips look like Os.
- Touch your right elbow to ask **O**ptions questions.
- Stomp your foot to remember **N**ext steps questions.

Bonus: *for coaching videos and a complete list of SOON coaching questions, visit* leaderlab.lifelabslearning.com

Let's take a look at the *SOON Funnel* in action. After her overwhelming conversation with Olivia wraps up, Mia hits the Do-Over Button and tries again:

Version 2: Do-Over

Olivia: You know Jeff, the finance team manager? Working with him is a nightmare. Every time I come to him with an issue, he makes it sound like it's *our* fault. I don't even have enough time to fix our issues, let alone his.

Mia: Sounds like two things, the issue with Jeff and the time issue. Which of those should we tackle first?

Olivia: Jeff, for sure.

Mia: I know it's been frustrating. <u>How do you think a **successful** relationship would look</u>?

Olivia: Well, I want him to take responsibility when problems arise.

Mia: That sounds reasonable. <u>What do you see as the **obstacles** standing in the way of that</u>?

Olivia: Him! He's honestly just rude.

Mia: Okay, so it might be a style or personality thing. What else comes to mind?

Olivia: Well, okay. If I zoom out to think about it, the other issue may be that he doesn't understand what our team does or why our issues are so time sensitive.

Mia: That sounds like something you have more control over than his personality, which is good. <u>What are some **options** you can think of, considering those obstacles</u>?

Olivia: Well, it may be good to put together some documentation to show him our workflow.

Mia: Great. What else comes to mind?

Olivia: I can also set up time with him to just talk things over.

Mia: What would you say?

Olivia: Maybe "Hey, I know we haven't gotten off to a strong start. Want to set up some time to learn more about each other's teams and chat about how best to work together?"

Mia: I love that. So you've got documentation and having a discussion as two good options. Would it be helpful to come up with more ideas?

Olivia: Actually, I think starting off with a conversation would be best.

Mia: Yeah, I agree. <u>In that case, what are your **next steps**</u>?

Olivia: I'll schedule a meeting with him right after our conversation.

Mia: Great! Let's debrief in our next one-on-one.

What made this coaching conversation so different from Mia's first attempt? In both cases, Mia asked high-quality questions, had a good variety of questions, and checked for clarity and understanding. But the first conversation was disorienting. The questions prompted ideas and insights, but they did not guide Olivia to analyze the problem systematically. That is the value of the *SOON Funnel*. In her coaching do-over, Mia helped Olivia leave with a plan.

Q-step into Coaching

The *SOON Funnel* represents the ideal coaching conversation. That said, the real world often limits the time we have to coach. Average managers treat this reality as an immovable obstacle, convinced they have no choice but to give directions and coach at some point "later" when there's time. But as venture capitalist Ben Horowitz has famously said, this habit collects "management debt." When we focus on the quick fix, we save time in the present, but we end up paying for it (with interest) in the future by returning to the same problem again and again.

The good news? The **Q-step** BU alone (from Chapter 1) works as a small but powerful coaching prompt when time is tight. Just **Pausing** to ask one question before going into Telling Mode helps people clarify their thinking and grow their problem-solving capacity putting those *4C* coaching moments to good use.

Practice Station

To level up your **Q-stepping** ability, let's do an exercise we introduced in Chapter 1, this time using some sample coaching moments. For each situation, consider what you would say if you went into the ever-tempting Telling Mode. Then, decide how you'd respond with a **Q-step**:

TELLING MODE	Q-STEP
I have no idea how to go about solving this problem. Can you help?	
Sample tell: Sure! I know exactly where to start. Let me show you.	Sample Q-steps: What is your goal? What have you tried so far? Where are you stuck?
Ugh. I never have enough time to get through all of my email. How does anyone do it?	
Sample tell: You have to set aside an hour in the morning to batch process email.	Sample Q-steps: What's important to you about that? When is it less of a problem?
This client is a nightmare. They're not happy with any of our revisions. How do I respond?	
Sample tell: You have to be firm but polite. Don't let them boss you around.	Sample Q-steps: What options have you considered? What are the pros and cons of each?

Q-step Q&A

Some managers are uncomfortable responding to a question with a **Q-step**, which creates an obstacle to coaching well. So, following are some of the most common Questions we get from our workshop participants, and quick Answers that will help you overcome each hurdle:

Q. What if my team member truly doesn't know the answer?

A. Coaching is about catalyzing insights based on existing knowledge. If it's someone's first day at work in your office and they ask, "Where is the bathroom?" it will do them little good if you **Q-step** by saying, "Where do you think the bathroom is?" There is plenty of information that should simply be one-directional rather than coached. For example, company history, strategy, policies, and requirements are all good things to tell. Be sure to reinforce people when they turn to you for help by **Validating** their decision. A simple, "Thanks for coming to me with that question," helps build a healthy question culture on your team.

Q. Won't it make me look incompetent if I look like I don't know the answer?

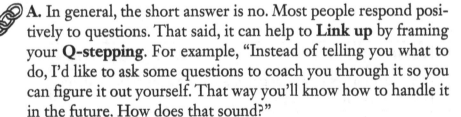

A. In general, the short answer is no. Most people respond positively to questions. That said, it can help to **Link up** by framing your **Q-stepping**. For example, "Instead of telling you what to do, I'd like to ask some questions to coach you through it so you can figure it out yourself. That way you'll know how to handle it in the future. How does that sound?"

Q. What if it's an emergency and there's no time to coach?

When there's a fire, we don't suggest you stop to ask, "Where do you think the fire extinguisher is?" if you already know. In times of true crisis, teams look to leaders for answers. But real and metaphorical fires aside, it's easy for our brains to see something as an emergency even when it's not. If time is limited, remember that a tiny **Pause** and a single **Q-step** (like "What are your thoughts?") still counts as coaching. When all else fails, you can Pause after the emergency is over to **Extract** the learning.

Q. Isn't it phony to ask a question when I already know the answer?

A. Usually, yes. And there's a fix for that. Commit to asking *authentic questions only*. Authentic questions are questions you genuinely want to know the answers to (rather than pseudo-questions, which are statements dressed up to look like questions).

Practice Station

Take a look at the pseudo-questions below, and decide how to convert each one to an authentic **Q-step** that lets both people learn:

PSEUDO-QUESTION	AUTHENTIC QUESTION
The customer success department asked me to help them interview candidates.	
Don't you think someone else should do that?	*How do you feel about that?*
I'm so sick of putting together this report every week. It's so draining.	
Have you thought about delegating it?	*What options have you considered?*

I'm thinking about switching my work hours to start two hours earlier.	
Why would you even think of that?	*What do you hope that would do?*

***

In summary: Coaching is the skill of catalyzing insights to accelerate competence, confidence, and motivation in others. Coach your team whenever your spot the *4C* coaching moments: Conundrums, Complaints, Confidence issues, and Completion. To become a better coach faster, use the LifeLabs Learning *SOON Funnel*: **S**uccess, **O**bstacles, **O**ptions, **N**ext steps (with **Playbacks** along the way). If you are short on time, even a single **Q-step** helps you leverage each coaching moment.

MY LAB REPORT	Today's Date:
My takeaways:	
I regularly coach others:	1 2 3 4 5 6 7 8 9 10 (strongly disagree) (strongly agree)
Experiment idea bank:	▪ If someone comes to me for advice, then I will Q-step by asking: "What are your thoughts?" ▪ If I'm helping someone solve a problem, I'll first ask, "What does success look like?" ▪ If someone commits to next steps, then I will write them down to create accountability.

MY LAB REPORT	Today's Date:
One small experiment I'll try to increase my score by 1 point:	
Post-experiment Learning Extractions:	

Bonus: Want to take your manager skills to the next level? Check out the bonus Inclusion Stations at leaderlab.lifelabs-learning.com.

My Learning Tracker

7 out of 7 Core BUs collected. 1 of 8 Core Skills collected.

Q-step	Playback	Deblur	Validate	Linkup	Pause	Extract
Coaching						

9

Feedback Skills

While coaching stood out in our research as the top skill of great managers, *feedback* was a very close runner-up. Thanks to our experience training thousands of managers through LifeLabs Learning, we know that feedback is also the skill that's most likely to make a manager's heart race and palms sweat. Perhaps for this reason, feedback is one of the biggest skill gaps we see among managers. On the bright side, it is also a powerful tipping point skill that impacts diverse domains like conflict resolution, teaching, meeting facilitation, and communication. So, even though many managers come to this topic with trepidation, they find that developing feedback skills leads to a rapid return on time invested (as well as significantly fewer sweaty palms). In this chapter, we'll share what feedback is, why it's important, and how to develop feedback skills faster, including how to (1) give feedback, (2) receive feedback, and (3) build a feedback culture on your team.

Practice Station
What is a piece of feedback you are hesitating to give someone? Jot it down here before you keep reading. By the end of this chapter, you'll know how to deliver this message well.

What Feedback Is (and Why It Matters)

Simply put, feedback is information that helps you adjust or maintain your behavior so that you can reach a goal. Thirst is feedback from your body letting you know you need hydration.

A knock is feedback from the door, letting you know your knuckles have hit it. And when it comes to the workplace, feedback is any information you receive that helps you become aware of the impact of your actions. Sometimes this feedback can come from results (for example, an increase in revenue is feedback that your sales campaign is working) and sometimes it has to come from people (for example, feedback from a coworker that your presentation was confusing).

If you and your team members existed within a predictable, unchanging environment, you would need very little feedback to know how you're doing. But in an environment that is ever-changing, ambiguous, and requires nonstop learning, frequent feedback becomes essential. Working in this type of environment without feedback is like trying to throw darts in the dark. Every once in a while, someone is bound to take a dart in the forehead. With feedback, you and your team can quickly learn, adjust, calibrate to one another's preferences, and reach your goals – even as they change.

How to Give Feedback Well

Take a look at the following conversation. It's pretty much a case study in what *not* to do when it comes to giving feedback. Mia didn't sleep well the night before; she's cranky, and it shows:

Version 1

Mia: Hey, we have to talk.
Luca: Um . . . okay.
Mia: The way you handled that client interaction is totally unacceptable.

Luca: What? Why?

Mia: You were so unprofessional!

Luca: I don't think I was unprofessional! I was polite the entire time.

Mia: Ugh. You're always so defensive. Don't you know we have a feedback culture?

Luca: It's not that I don't want feedback . . . .

Mia: Okay, good. My feedback is this: don't tell clients something is their fault. Even if they were the ones who made a mistake, we shouldn't make them feel bad about it.

Oh, Mia. This wasn't one of her finest manager moments. Luckily, she has her Do-Over Button at the ready. First, we'll break down the components of effective feedback so you can develop your feedback skills faster, then we'll travel back in time with Mia to watch her try again.

So what does it take to deliver feedback well in even the toughest of situations? When we studied managers who were nominated as the best feedback givers at their companies, we found that they did just about the opposite of what Mia did with Luca. We noticed so many commonalities among these great managers that we've summed up the four essential components of any feedback message in a model we call the *Q-BIQ Method* (pronounced *cubic*). You can remember this tool by thinking of cubic measurement (a measure of capacity) since giving great feedback increases individual and team capacity.

Q-BIQ stands for **Question, Behavior, Impact, Question.** We love this model because we see it transform our workshop participants' feedback quality from average to great in a matter of minutes. So, let's examine each part of the *Q-BIQ Method* one at a time, then put it all together.

Q-BIQ Method Part 1: Question

Q-BIQ Method			
Question	Behavior	Impact	Question

By now, you probably won't be surprised to hear that the best feedback conversations start with a *question*. One of the most brain-friendly **Q-steps** is what we call a *Micro-Yes*. For example:

- "Would you be up for hearing my thoughts on your presentation?"
- "Can I give you my feedback on the product launch?"
- "Is now a good time to debrief about how that meeting went?"

Why does a Micro-Yes question lead to more effective feedback? First, it prepares people. Surprise and mystery intensify emotions (Luna and Renninger 2015), so unexpected criticism feels worse than feedback we're expecting. In the feedback exchange between Mia and Luca, Mia gets close to a Micro-Yes, but doesn't quite make it. "We have to talk," or even its close cousin "Can we talk?" can strike fear into the bravest of hearts – making people instantly assume someone is breaking up with them, firing them, or something similarly drastic. Without clarity about the topic, people show up to the conversation defensive rather than prepared. Even when it comes to praise, which tends to be easier for our brains to process, readying ourselves leads to more learning.

A Micro-Yes question also makes people more receptive to feedback by signaling that it is a two-way conversation. When you give others shared power in this way, you greatly reduce the likelihood of triggering that pesky amygdala hijack we talked about in Chapter 6. The point here is not to trick folks into hearing your feedback but to give genuine choice over whether and/or when to hear the feedback. If the person says no to your

Micro-Yes, great. It means you found out early that they wouldn't have been receptive and saved both of you the time and struggle.

If you think the feedback will greatly benefit you, them, or others, you can always **Q-steps** with "When would be a better time?" or "Would you be willing to tell me what makes you uninterested in hearing the feedback?" And if the feedback is mandatory (like in the case of underperformance or misaligned expectations), give choice in the "when" instead of the "whether." For example, "I'd like us to discuss the missed goal to make sure we're aligned on expectations and have a plan of action. When would work well for you this week?"

Q-BIQ Method Part 2: Behavior

Q-BIQ Method			
Question	**Behavior**	Impact	Question

Once your feedback recipient consents to the conversation, describe the specific *behavior* that you believe had a helpful or harmful impact. The trick to giving great feedback is to focus only on *behavior that a camera can capture.* The biggest feedback pitfall is using "blur words" (see Chapter 3), words that mean different things to different people. The most common blur words that creep up in feedback conversations include:

Blur words that describe a **person rather than a behavior.** *For example, a camera can't tell if someone is "thoughtful," but it can observe someone wishing you a happy birthday.*

Blur words that **generalize.** *For example, while a camera can detect that someone is "always" late, it is highly unlikely that this behavior actually always happens.*

Blur words that make **assumptions** about people's thoughts, feelings, or intentions. *For example, a camera can't tell if you're "not listening" but it can observe that you are looking at your phone.*

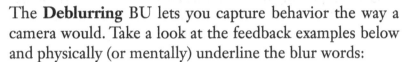

Practice Station

The **Deblurring** BU lets you capture behavior the way a camera would. Take a look at the feedback examples below and physically (or mentally) underline the blur words:

- *You are so inconsiderate! You constantly dismiss people when they bring up new ideas.*
- *I just love how creative you are! Your client presentations always have that wow factor.*
- *You're not putting in enough effort. Your completion rate is much worse than average.*

Here are the feedback examples again with the blur words underlined:

- *You are <u>so inconsiderate</u>! You <u>constantly dismiss people</u> when they bring up new ideas.*
- *I just love how <u>creative</u> you are! Your client presentations <u>always</u> have that <u>wow factor</u>.*
- *You're not putting in <u>enough effort</u>. Your <u>completion rate</u> is <u>much worse</u> than <u>average</u>.*

Now, try converting these blurry pieces of feedback into behaviors that a camera could capture. You'll see our samples in the right column. Come up with at least one of your own for each example:

BLURRY	DEBLURRED BEHAVIOR
You are <u>so inconsiderate</u>! You <u>constantly dismiss people</u> when they bring up new ideas.	*I noticed when the intern suggested an idea in yesterday's team meeting, you rolled your eyes and said, "That will never work."*

BLURRY	DEBLURRED BEHAVIOR
I love how <u>creative</u> you are! Your client presentations <u>always</u> have that <u>wow factor</u>.	*I love that you used full-screen images and videos in your client presentation!*
You're not putting in <u>enough effort</u>. Your <u>response time</u> is <u>much worse</u> than <u>average</u>.	*In this past month, your response time was 30 minutes, and our team standard is 10 minutes.*

To convert your blur words to behaviors, ask yourself:

- "What led me to this opinion?"
- "What specifically did this person do or say?"
- "What would a camera capture?"

While it's essential to **Pause** and **Deblur** your feedback rather than blurting it out, don't wait too long. Deliver your feedback within a week to keep the behavior from blurring in everyone's memory. If you're worried that a one-time occurrence isn't a "real" issue, use a framing statement, like "I've only noticed this once, and I don't want to make it bigger than it is, but I want to point it out while it's still a small issue."

And whatever you do, *do not sandwich your feedback*. Despite the fact that many corners of the Internet will tell you feedback is best delivered in a combination of praise/critique/praise (also known as the "shit sandwich"), research confirms that this approach generally results in confusion and reduced trust (Bressler and Von Bergen 2014). The most nutritious feedback is small, bite-sized snacks, delivered frequently. If you have praise *and* criticism to share about one thing, give your feedback recipient a choice of the order. For example, "There were things I liked about the class and things I didn't like. Which should I focus on first?" If you're still tempted to sandwich because you're concerned direct feedback may sound harsh, try starting with a **Validation** statement. For example: "I care about our relationship, so I'm sharing this feedback because I hope it can help us work better together."

If you did not observe the behavior firsthand, do not fall into the *triangulation trap*. Triangulation is what happens when someone delivers third-party feedback that they didn't personally observe. Few things feel worse than hearing about negative things "others" have said about you. To bust up triangulation, encourage people to go directly to the source – coaching them and sharing the *Q-BIQ Method*. If that doesn't work, offer to join the conversation to help it go smoothly. And if this option isn't possible either, offer to keep an eye out for the behavior so you can deliver feedback from your own perspective, if you happen to observe it.

Q-BIQ Method Part 3: Impact

Q-BIQ Method			
Question	Behavior	**Impact**	Question

 Once you've described the behavior, it's time to use the **Linkup** BU (from Chapter 5) to explain the *impact* of the person's behavior. Without an impact statement, feedback holds little meaning and doesn't catalyze motivation for repeating or reducing the behavior. Here are some examples of the Micro-Yes question, behavior, and impact statements combined:

- Is now a good time to share feedback about the event? I see you accommodated all our dietary restrictions, and I bring it up because my team feels so included at the event.
- Can we chat about new hire training? I noticed you haven't offered to lead any of them. I wanted to call it out because

you've mentioned wanting to be in a leadership role, and I think this experience can help you build skills that would make you a stronger candidate.

- Can I offer some feedback on your client communication? I appreciate that you've been sending weekly progress updates to clients. The reason I think it's so helpful is that they can ask more useful questions now, which lets us all make faster progress.

If something is bugging you but you're not quite sure why, hold off on delivering the feedback. Determine the **Linkup** so your feedback recipient can come up with solutions that meet your underlying needs. once you do deliver the feedback, make sure you **Link up** to impact that is meaningful to your feedback recipient. For example, some people will be most moved when you point out their impact on you, some will care more about the team or end users, and others might be more motivated if the impact is on them. Let's say you want to deliver feedback on a meeting. Notice how the impact statement changes depending on the recipient's primary motivator:

Their Motivator:	Feedback Example: *I noticed you prepared prereading materials and an agenda.*
Personal growth	*I mention it because I know you've been working on your meeting skills, and this was such a great example of a well-run meeting!*
Team support	*I mention it because it allowed everyone on the team to feel included and prepared, and to show up with their best ideas.*
End-user impact	*I mention it because it helped us make rapid progress in the meeting, which means our users will be able to benefit from getting those new features faster.*

If the consequences of the person's behavior are severe (like a demotion or dismissal), the impact statement is a good place to make that clear. For example, "I see your average response time is 30 minutes. I bring it up because a 10-minute response time is a requirement for this role. If you don't hit that goal by the end of the month, you'll be asked to leave, so I want to do whatever I can to help you succeed."

On the other hand, if the feedback you share is subjective, frame it as a hypothesis. For example, "I noticed when you reviewed Quinn's proposal, you shared what you disliked and nothing about what you liked. I may be wrong here, but I mention it because I got the sense they left that meeting demotivated. What was your impression?" If you find yourself in a disagreement about the validity of your feedback, come up with ways to test your hypothesis. For example, gather data, track results, or ask for other people's perspectives.

Q-BIQ Method Part 4: Question

Q-BIQ Method			
Question	Behavior	Impact	**Question**

The final piece of the feedback puzzle is a return to our good friend the *question*. Great feedback is a two-way conversation. It is an exercise of collective meaning-making where people bring their perceptions together. So once you've shared your message, remember to **Q-step**. Here are some sample questions you can ask to invite your feedback recipient into the conversation:

- "What are your thoughts?"
- "How do you see it?"
- "Does that resonate with you?"

 When you end your feedback with a question and a **Pause**, you signal that you care about the other person's perspective, increasing their likelihood of changing their behavior. In some cases, your question will launch a valuable coaching conversation that lets you help the feedback recipient come up with ways to apply your feedback. In other cases, it will shine a light on fuzzy expectations and disagreements. Sometimes you will pool your perspectives or find a middle ground. Other times it might be perfectly fine to disagree.

To avoid miscommunication, wrap up your conversation by agreeing to next steps. We often hear from our workshop participants that they gave perfect feedback only to find that nothing changed. To avoid this, wrap up your feedback conversations with the N of the *SOON Funnel* and write it down for even greater accountability. For example, "So we both know what to expect, would you share how you see the next steps? I'll jot it down in our one-on-one doc so we're on the same page."

Practice Station

Let's put it all together. Following are a couple of examples of feedback delivered using the *Q-BIQ Method*. To make this tool even easier to remember, we use the feedback template "*I noticed that . . . I mention it because . . .*" But when you put this tool to use, use any language that feels most natural to you:

Question	Behavior	Impact	Question
Can I share my reaction to your announcement?	**I noticed that** you gave credit to each person on the team.	**I mention it because** I felt valued and motivated.	How did you manage to keep track of everyone involved?

Would you be open to hearing my thoughts on your presentation?	**I noticed that** each slide had several sentences of text.	**I mention it because** I found myself reading rather than fully listening.	What do you think?

Your turn! Write the feedback message you thought about at the start of this chapter:

Question	Behavior	Impact	Question

Bonus: For feedback videos and to download the Q-BIQ Feedback Prep Grid, visit leaderlab.lifelabslearning.com.

***

Now, let's return to that cringey feedback conversation we shared earlier. It's time for Mia to hit the Do-Over Button and try again using the *Q-BIQ Method:*

Version 2: Do-Over

Mia: Hey, I'd like to share some feedback with you about that client interaction. When would be a good time to chat?

Luca: Oh, now is fine.

Mia: Are you sure? There's something I wanted to point out while it's still fresh on my mind, but it's not urgent.

Luca: Yeah. I want to hear.

Mia: Okay, thanks! I noticed when the client explained her problem, you pointed out that she didn't read the contract carefully. You're right that it was her mistake, but I mention it because she might have gotten the impression we didn't take responsibility, plus we didn't help her solve her problem. What do you think?

Luca: I get that. I don't want clients feeling bad. But I also don't want anyone thinking we screwed up. It was her mistake, not ours.

Mia: Yeah. Sounds like you want clients to know we do high-quality work.

Luca: Yes, definitely.

Mia: Okay, great. Me too. So what comes to mind for you as a possible solution for how to handle this kind of situation in the future?

Notice that none of the elements of the *Q-BIQ Method* include giving advice. Many people use the word "feedback" interchangeably with the word "advice," but they are different concepts.

Feedback = I observe something you might not be aware of + I bring it to your awareness + *you* decide what to do.

For example, "I noticed you spoke several times in the meeting and most people didn't speak up at all, so we might be missing important perspectives. What do you think?"

Advice = I observe something you might not be aware of + *I* tell you what to do instead.

For example, "I suggest you talk less in our meetings. Something you can try is waiting until everyone else has spoken before you chime in with your ideas."

Why does this distinction matter? Just like coaching, feedback provides the best development, motivation, and commitment opportunity when the recipient decides on their own next steps. This doesn't mean that great managers never give advice. It means they default to giving their team members opportunities to come to their own conclusions first. (That's our advice, anyway.)

How to Receive Feedback Well

It can be tempting to focus all your energy on delivering feedback well and ignore the skill of *receiving* feedback. This is a mistake. Leaders who give feedback like feedback superstars but don't make it easy for others to give *them* feedback miss out on a major opportunity for learning *and* for teaching. Great managers make it enjoyable for others to give them feedback, so they keep getting even better because they receive feedback often. In the meanwhile, they also set the standard for their team for how to be great feedback recipients.

So how can you receive feedback well? First, adopt a mind-set that authors Douglas Stone and Sheila Heen (2014) call the "second score." The "first score" is the one your feedback givers already assigned to you based on something you did. This score is in the past now, and you can't control it. What you *can* control is the "second score" they give you on how well you receive their feedback. To ace that second score, it's not enough to say "Thanks!" and go about your day. Receiving feedback skillfully includes the following steps:

1. **Play back** what you hear so you fully understand the feedback.

   For example, "Thank you for coming to me with that! Let me play it back to make sure I fully understood. I heard you say _____. Is that right?"

2. Step back to **Q-step**. Ask what led to their perspective (pulling for behavior and impact).

   For example, "So that I can see where you're coming from, would you share an example? What about _____ is important to you?"

3. **Play back** to show you've understood their perspective.

   For example, "Got it. So it sounds like the situation was _____. Did I get that right?"

4. **Step forward** to explore how you can apply their feedback in the future.

   For example, "Okay, so based on your feedback, I think I can do _____ moving forward. How does that sound?" Or "I'm struggling to come up with ways to apply this feedback. Can we think of some solutions together? My concern is _____. What do you think?" For best results, include (genuine) **Validation** *statements in your reply. For example: "Thanks for talking to me about this," "I can see why you'd feel that way," and "I'm eager to figure out a fix." These small signals help reduce your feedback giver's anxiety and make them more willing to share feedback in the future.*

Practice Station

Want a playful way to remember the four steps of receiving feedback well? Think of it as the *Feedback Salsa* (as in the dance, not the delicious condiment).

1. **Playback:** Begin in what dancers call the "starting position" – stand together, fully aligned.

2. **Step back: Q-step** to understand *past* behavior that led to their perspective.

3. **Playback:** Get aligned on a shared reality.

4. **Step forward:** Explore ideas for how to apply their feedback in the *future*.

If you're noticing that your brain is going into defensive mode, **Pause** between each step until you're ready to move on. You don't have to break out into an actual dance whenever you get feedback. (Then again, doing that might make you an even more popular feedback target.)

Source: LifeLabs Learning.

How to Build a Feedback Culture Faster

Before we wrap up, let's briefly address one more feedback skill of great managers. Feedback mastery isn't just about the short-term exchange of feedback but also about building a lasting feedback culture. When you make giving, receiving, and asking for feedback a norm on your team, you enable everyone to learn faster, collaborate better, and do great work. Here are three ways great managers build a feedback culture.

1. Offer More Praise Than Criticism

Though many people assume "feedback" is code for criticism, the most frequent type of feedback on high-performing teams is actually praise. Great managers and teams constantly **Pause** to point out what they see others doing well. Not only does this kind of recognition lead to more engagement, but it also builds confidence and helps people strengthen their strengths. Plus, research shows that employees who aren't satisfied with how often they receive praise at work are 300% more likely to say they'll quit in the following year (Robison 2006). To create a feedback culture faster, start giving specific praise on a daily basis.

2. Pull for Feedback Often

The next important aspect of an enduring feedback culture is a version of the **Extract** BU (from Chapter 7): pull for feedback rather than waiting for it to be "pushed" to you. This pulling habit functions as an important signal-setting action. It's a cue for your team that this is a place where feedback is valued and expected all around. What's more, research shows that leaders who ask for critical feedback are perceived as more effective (Ashford and Tsui 2017). When we asked the great managers we studied to share their feedback pulling secrets with us, we collected the following tips:

- **Be specific.** When you say, "Got any feedback?" most people draw a blank or feel too intimidated to be honest. Make it easier for them by **Deblurring** your request. For example, "Would you share feedback with me on how our one-on-one meetings are going?"
- **Linkup.** Explain why you're looking for feedback so people are motivated to share. For example, "So that I can keep improving our new hire experience, would you share what you think went well with your onboarding and what could have been better?"
- **Keep it small.** Some people will worry about giving their manager feedback no matter how sincere you are. Make the request smaller by using something we call the "10% question": "What's one thing I can improve about_____ by 10%?"
- **Follow up.** After you've implemented the feedback, let the feedback giver know about the positive impact it had. This inspires people to give you feedback more often, and shows how valuable feedback can be.

3. Create Feedback Touchpoints

The last part of the feedback culture equation is creating feedback touchpoints. A touchpoint acts as a helpful **Pause** point and nudge to catalyze feedback conversations even when you're not around. Here are two examples of effective feedback touchpoints:

- **Schedule retros:** Retro, retrospective, post-mortem, debrief, after-action review – these sessions go by many names, but they are all fundamentally the same process of **Extracting** the learning from the past to apply it in the future. Some common retro questions include "What went well?" "What didn't go well?" "What can we do differently next time?" Research shows that surgical teams that debrief together after each surgery quickly improve patient satisfaction and make fewer surgical errors (Marks et al. 2014). So, schedule retros after projects, collaborations, or on a quarterly basis. Also, should you ever need surgery, ask your medical team if they do retros.

- **Make public praise easy:** Make it simple and fun for your team to **Pause** and share praise with one another. Create a visual space (physically or digitally) to recognize one another's efforts and achievements, share gratitude, and pass on kudos from internal and external users. Praise is helpful, feels great, and helps create a positive association with feedback.

In summary: Feedback lets us learn faster and collaborate better. Great feedback follows the *Q-BIQ Method:* **Question** → **Behavior** → **Impact** → **Question**. **Deblur** the behavior and **Link up** to impact that matters most to the feedback recipient- then **Q-step** to hear their perspective. Receive feedback well, using **Validation** statements and the *Feedback Salsa* so people are more likely to keep sharing their thoughts, and help build a strong feedback culture on your team.

MY LAB REPORT	Today's Date:
My takeaways:	
I regularly give feedback:	1 2 3 4 5 6 7 8 9 10 (strongly disagree) (strongly agree)
Experiment idea bank:	• If I notice someone doing something well, then I will give them feedback. • If I am new to working with someone, then I will ask how they like to exchange feedback. • If it is Friday, then I will ask for feedback.
One small experiment I'll try to increase my score by 1 point:	
Post-experiment Learning Extractions:	

Bonus: Want to take your manager skills to the next level? Check out the bonus Inclusion Stations at leaderlab.lifelabs-learning.com.

My Learning Tracker

7 out of 7 Core BUs collected. 2 of 8 Core Skills collected.

Q-step	Playback	Deblur	Validate	Linkup	Pause	Extract
Coaching	Feedback					

10

Productivity Skills

Let's say you ask someone how they manage their money, and they laugh, shake their head, and reply: "I never know where exactly it's going. I don't know how best to spend it. And I never have enough." This would be a bleak response. And yet, when it comes to managing time, these are precisely the types of answers we hear from people in our workshops. Not only do folks struggle to figure out how to use time (their most scarce and precious resource), but they've often totally given up on the idea that a strategic use of time is even possible.

The good news? By studying what great managers do differently, we've seen that getting out of time debt is possible and even enjoyable. It just takes a deliberate commitment to mastering *productivity skills* and passing on these skills to your team. These productivity skills also tip over into better decision-making, strategic thinking, delegation, meeting facilitation, and planning.

To begin, take a look at the following conversation:

Version 1

Mia: Hey, how's the project coming along?
Olivia: Ugh. I've barely managed to make any progress.
Mia: Oh, no. I thought things were starting to get better.
Olivia: They were, but now my inbox is taking over my life.
Mia: Yeah, it's been so busy, even with Kofi joining the team. How realistic is it to meet the deadline we had set?

> **Olivia:** I mean, I know I can get my part of it done. I'll just work over the weekend. But I have no idea if everyone else will get their part done. Things are better with Jeff in Finance, but they have their own fires to put out, so I don't know how seriously they're taking my requests. Besides, the last two projects we worked on ended up getting scrapped, so I think they're not very motivated to help out, and I don't want to sour our relationship again.

Situations like these can leave managers and their teams overwhelmed. Luckily, we've found that the vast majority of productivity challenges fall into just four categories. Knowing these categories will allow you to quickly diagnose and resolve issues for yourself and your team, making your life easier, and helping you become an even better manager faster. What are the top four productivity challenges? We'll list each one along with their most common symptoms. See if you recognize yourself or any of your team members within this list:

Productivity Challenge	Symptoms
1. Time awareness: knowing where time is going, how much time something will take, and how to communicate time to others	*Chronic lateness, missed deadlines, meetings starting late or running too long*
2. Prioritization: identifying the most important thing in a sea of important things	*Being too busy, overperfecting work, spending time on work that should be delegated to others*

(continued)

Productivity Challenge	Symptoms
3. Organization: having an efficient system for getting things done	*Missed commitments, worrying about things slipping through the cracks, searching for notes or to-do items*
4. Focus: stay on task without in-terruptions	*Frequent context switching, getting distracted, rarely feeling a sense of flow*

Practice Station

Take two minutes now to diagnose each person on your team. Which of the four challenge areas above describes their biggest productivity challenge?

While there are countless productivity hacks and tools – many of them with an impassioned fanbase of self-proclaimed productivity nerds – helping your team members find the right solution faster starts by **Pausing** to identify the root cause of their productivity problems. In the same way that there's no such thing as the "best" medicine, selecting the right productivity tool is dependent on making the right diagnosis. So, keep your diagnoses in mind as we share an array of productivity tools you can pass onto your team (and model using yourself).

Now back to Mia. Recognizing that she's still unclear about the source of Olivia's productivity problems, she decides to try again. Notice how she **Q-steps** with diagnostic questions in this do-over conversation and try to diagnose Olivia's challenges:

Version 2: Do-Over

Mia: Hey, how's the project coming along?

Olivia: Ugh. I've barely managed to make any progress.

Mia: How far along did you hope to be at this point?

Olivia: I wanted to be about 50% done by now, and I'm barely at 10%. I can still make the deadline, but I have to make much faster progress.

Mia: That's tough. What do you think is getting in your way?

Olivia: Well, my inbox is taking over my life lately. And when I'm not responding to email, I'm stuck in a meeting. If I'm not in a meeting, I'm dealing with some kind of emergency.

Mia: Oof. Okay. Let's figure this out. <u>Mind if I ask some questions so we can figure out the root of the problem together?</u>

Olivia: Not at all. I would appreciate it. It's like I keep coming back to this situation.

Mia: Okay, so let's touch on time awareness first. <u>How clear are you about where your time is going and how long things take you?</u>

Olivia: Hmm. I'm clear about that, for the most part. The only exception is email. I'm responding to email all day, so I have no idea how much time I'm spending there.

Mia: Got it. How about when it comes to prioritization? <u>How clear are you about what's most important to do and what's okay to delay</u>?

Olivia: I mean, at this point, everything I'm doing is top priority. There isn't really an option of something I can just *not* do – especially if it's client stuff.

Mia: Are you seeing all clients as equally high priority?

Olivia: Well, in the past we've treated them all the same, but the truth is there are some really tiny accounts that are also the most time-consuming.

Mia: That would be good to talk about some more. But first, I'm also curious about organization. <u>How efficient would you say your workflow is on a scale of one to ten</u>?

Olivia: That part is solid. I'd give it a nine. I always know what I have to get done. There's just not enough time to do it.

Mia: Sounds like you have a strong foundation to build on. That's great. And last question – <u>how happy are you with how focused you are at work</u>?

Olivia: Oh, that part is horrible. I'm checking email while I'm in the middle of everything else, so I'm constantly context switching. It's exhausting.

You may have noticed that Olivia is struggling with multiple productivity issues, but prioritization is likely at the core. It could be tempting for Mia to simply recommend her favorite productivity tool (we bet you have one of those too), but the crucial first move is picking just one productivity challenge to tackle. It doesn't have to be the perfect place to start, but it should be one  that will provide a meaningful sense of progress and the fuel to keep improving. Once you've used **Q-steps** and **Playbacks** to **Deblur** the primary challenge (time awareness, prioritization, organization, or focus), offer a productivity tool or framework that best matches the need. Let's examine the most effective tools for each challenge area. Again, you might be tempted to use or advertise them all at once, but keep in mind that a one-at-a-time approach results in more productivity faster.

Time Awareness

Pop quiz!

- Do you know what time it is right now – without checking?
- How long have you been reading this chapter so far?
- Think of an item on your to-do list. How long will it take you to get it done?

An interesting characteristic of the most productive managers we've studied is that they are very aware of time. They treat it as a real, important, and finite resource and pass on this "time integrity" to their teams and coworkers. Here are our three favorite tools for quickly increasing your and your team's time awareness:

Time Awareness Tool #1: Use Time Language

One interesting finding we came across in our observations of great managers and teams is how they talk about time. Try to spot the patterns when comparing the following two conversations:

Average team	Highly productive team
Mia: Shall we move onto the last item on the agenda? **Luca:** Yeah, but before that, I have a quick question. Should we still meet next week even though most people will be out on vacation? **Olivia:** If we're not meeting, we should tell the client ASAP since they planned to join. **Mia:** Let's decide at some point this week so it doesn't come as a surprise for the client. **Olivia:** It'll take like two seconds to alert them.	**Mia:** In our last ten minutes, shall we move onto the final item on the agenda? **Luca:** Actually, I think I have an item that's more pressing. It should take five minutes. **Mia:** Anyone have an objection to moving our last agenda item to the parking lot? **Luca:** Thanks. I'm realizing two of us will be out next week. Shall we still meet? **Olivia:** If we don't, we should let the client know by five p.m. today. I can send the email.

The conversation on the left is littered with time "blur words." Did you catch them all? In one short exchange, the team managed to say: "quick question," "ASAP," "some point this week," and "two seconds." These time blur words are common, and represent a loose relationship with time. By contrast, the team on the right uses precise *time language*. Research shows that simply talking about time increases time awareness and improves performance (Janicik and Bartel 2003).

To adopt a *time language* norm, you can share your explicit commitment to time integrity or simply start **Deblurring** time. For example, when someone asks you if you have "one moment," you can say, "I have five minutes right now or we can discuss it in our one-on-one. Which do you prefer?" If someone asks for a favor, promising that "it will take you no time at all," you can gently bring time awareness into the conversation by saying, "I want to make sure I can follow through if I say yes. Can I ask some questions to make sure I have enough time to help?" You can also help improve productivity faster by getting your team in the habit of making time predictions. Ask, "How long do you think this will take?" then help **Extract** the learning by asking, "How long did it end up taking?"

Keep in mind that our relationship with time is highly influenced by culture. So if people on your team treat time differently, don't take lateness or an insistence on timeliness as a sign of disrespect. Make time to align on your time norms together, including when precision matters and when a more fluid approach to time is just fine.

Time Awareness Tool #2: Start and Stop Meetings on Time

One of the most effective things a manager can do to create shared time awareness is to simply *start and stop meetings on time*. Not only does this behavior have a positive domino effect on the rest of your organization, but it is also a signal-setting action that establishes time integrity as a norm rather than an occasional pleasant surprise. As simple as this behavior sounds, managers often struggle to implement it. In fact, meeting researcher Steven Rogelberg found that about 50% of meetings start late, and late meetings tend to have worse outcomes (Rogelberg 2019). Want to guess the main reason for this widespread tardiness? Other people's meetings ending late! Below are some of our favorite solutions:

- Start on time, even if few participants are present.
- Ask people to assign time estimates to each agenda item.
- Designate a timekeeper and/or use an audible timer to keep everyone on track.
- Put a clock in the room or add a countdown on the digital screen.

- Lock the door (physically or digitally) once the meeting starts, making it impossible for late participants to join. We learned this approach from an executive team that struggled with lateness – leading to many expensive wasted minutes spent waiting. They agreed to lock their (glass) door :01 past the hour, which made for many amusing moments of watching people dash down the hall and attempt to pry open the conference room door. Their year-long lateness streak ended within a week.

Time Awareness Tool #3: Suggest Doing a Time Audit

The final time awareness tool we highly recommend to increase productivity faster is helping your team members do *time audits*. Much like an expense tracker, fitness tracker, or sleep tracker, a *time audit* makes your reality visible so you can **Extract** insights and make more informed decisions. This is an excellent practice to encourage since research shows that people consistently underestimate how long things take – a phenomenon known in psychology as the "planning fallacy" (Buehler, Griffin, and Ross 1994).

You can choose one of countless *time audit* apps or use a simple spreadsheet. We recommend encouraging your team members to see where their time goes for at least one week, **Pausing** briefly to track activities in 30-minute intervals either at the end of every day or several times a day. We do *not* recommend using *time audits* as a micromanaging tool – having each person report exactly how they are using their time. Instead, offer it up as a tool to use alone or share with you and the team as a way to optimize time use together. As long as it is not a pattern of behavior, if your team members sometimes confess to bad time management, **Validate** their willingness to share so they keep coming to you for help. For example, say: "It's great you're showing me your time audit even if it was a rough week. This way we can figure this out together." Here is a sample *time audit* format you can suggest:

Time	Activity	Planned/ Reactive	Energized/ Drained
8:00 a.m.–8:30 a.m.	Checked email	Reactive	Neutral
8:30 a.m.–9:00 a.m.	Helped coworker	Reactive	Energized
9:00 a.m –9:30 a.m.	Finance meeting	Planned	Drained
9:30 a.m.–10:00 a.m.	Finance meeting	Planned	Drained

Bonus: Download a *time audit* template at leaderlab.lifelabslearning.com.

***

Simply tracking time alone can be a treasure trove of information for you, your team members, and your team as a whole. While you're at it, you can also **Extract** additional information like whether each activity was planned (scheduled for this time) or reactive (unplanned). You can also add in a measure of whether each item felt energizing, draining, or neutral. Once the data collection is done, you can **Q-step** and ask coaching questions like these:

- "Did anything surprise you?"
- "Are there activities you should make time for proactively in the future?"
- "Are there activities you can batch-process/consolidate to be more efficient?"
- "Are there certain times of the day you are more productive than other times?"
- "Are some of us doing certain tasks much faster or slower? How can we learn from each other or better distribute responsibilities?"

One significant insight many people have when they complete a *time audit* is that not all hours of the day are created equal. For example, research shows that some people have a productivity spike in the morning and some tend to do their best creative work in the evening (Pope 2016; Wieth and Zacks 2011). Armed with *time audit* data, you can help people rearrange how they spend their day, moving their toughest or highest-priority work to their brains' best windows of time, finding ways to improve efficiency, and no longer ending the week "time broke."

Prioritization

One of the saddest things we've come across in our research on productivity is that some of the hardest-working people are also some of the least productive. How can this be? It's simple: our brains have not evolved to prioritize long-term benefits. Left unchecked, your team members move from one task to the next, doing the easiest things, the things someone asked them to do, or simply the things right in front of them. Especially as stress increases, prioritization effectiveness declines. In one study of 43,000 encounters of doctors and patients, researchers found that when the workload was heaviest, physicians prioritized their easiest cases, leaving the most severe cases to wait the longest – a tendency known as "completion bias" (Gino and Staats 2016). Among all professions, it can be easy to get sucked into an endless stream of activities that *feel* like progress but that leave tomorrow looking much like yesterday.

Too often, employees don't **Pause** to question if they were spending their time wisely, and there is little alignment on which activities are the best use of time. On the other hand, teams led by the great managers we studied had a stronger sense of clarity, confidence, and progress (even if they physically worked fewer hours). These teams were often able to get more accomplished than similar teams with more resources because they wasted less time. The interesting thing is that even when these teams made mistakes in their priorities, they were still more successful because they could quickly learn and change course. So, what does it take to help your team prioritize well? Here are three tools we love:

Prioritization Tool #1: Ask About MITs

The first prioritization tool we'll share is the easiest to implement and will improve your team members' productivity the fastest: ask them to name their Most Important Things, *MITs*. You can **Q-step** about *MITs* as a coaching question in your one-on-ones, start daily team meetings with an *MIT* review, or use *MITs* as a tool to align on priorities with your team, manager, and other leaders across the organization (or Extract lessons about why you're misaligned). Help your team members **Pause** to name their *MITs* when they find themselves mired in endless emails, messages, requests, and to-do list items or simply when they're unsure what to do first (and be sure to **Playback** what you hear). And you can use *MITs* to guide longer-term planning by asking, "What are your *MITs* this month? How about this quarter?" "And which company *MIT* does this **Linkup** to?"

Help limit the *MITs* to three items at most. After all, the essence of prioritization is having a much shorter to-do list than a to-not-do list. In fact, the word "decide" comes from the Latin *decidere*, meaning "to cut off." To prioritize well, we must be willing to cut off what we *won't* do to focus on what we *will* do. Research shows that companies with fewer firmwide priorities report higher revenue growth (Leinwand and Mainardi 2011).

Prioritization Tool #2: Use the Quadrant Method

Sometimes just asking people to **Pause** and name their *MITs* is enough to clarify how they should use their time. But other times, the relative values of different tasks are more ambiguous. For these situations, many of the great managers we studied used some version of a *Quadrant Method*. This is a prioritization technique first introduced by U.S. President Dwight Eisenhower, then popularized by author Stephen Covey.

To use the *Quadrant Method* with your team, draw four quadrants with "importance" on the Y axis and "urgency" along the X. The distinction between urgency and importance alone is valuable to clarify with your team. Urgency means time pressure (for example, deadlines or scheduled meetings). Importance means adding long-term value to the organization (for example, developing skill capacity or inventing new systems). If you don't **Deblur** these concepts, it can become easy for your team to operate solely based on urgency. Here is the version of the *Quadrant Method* we've found most helpful:

Quadrant 1: Fires	Quadrant 2: Investments
More Urgent & More Important	Less Urgent & More Important
Big client canceling, homepage crash, high-performer quitting	*Giving feedback, having one-on-one, improving process, developing new skill*
Quadrant 3: Deception	**Quadrant 4: Recharge**
More Urgent & Less Important	Less Urgent & Less Important
Low-value *email and meetings, perfecting a presentation, doing work you could have delegated*	*Taking breaks, moving/ stretching, chatting with coworkers*

If you're already a fan of the *Quadrant Method*, you may have noticed that the LifeLabs Learning version refers to Quadrant 4 as the "Recharge Quadrant" rather than its typical designation as the "Trash Quadrant." We've rebranded this quadrant because, while the activities here usually don't directly **Linkup** to organizational goals, they can serve as bursts of fuel to power other work. Counterintuitive as it sounds, the most productive teams do spend time in Quadrant 4, and the great managers we studied model **Pausing** to take this time (see Chapter 6).

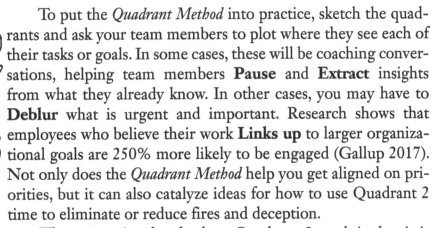

To put the *Quadrant Method* into practice, sketch the quadrants and ask your team members to plot where they see each of their tasks or goals. In some cases, these will be coaching conversations, helping team members **Pause** and **Extract** insights from what they already know. In other cases, you may have to **Deblur** what is urgent and important. Research shows that employees who believe their work **Links up** to larger organizational goals are 250% more likely to be engaged (Gallup 2017). Not only does the *Quadrant Method* help you get aligned on priorities, but it can also catalyze ideas for how to use Quadrant 2 time to eliminate or reduce fires and deception.

The one major drawback to Quadrant 2 work is that it is easy to keep deprioritizing since it often doesn't have a true deadline. Quadrant 1 is like racing to the dentist with a terrible toothache. Quadrant 2 is scheduling biannual dental cleanings. A toothache is hard to ignore. Cleanings are easy to put off. So what do unusually productive people do differently? Researcher Dan Ariely has found that they practice the simple habit of "calendar blocking." In other words, they take their Quadrant 2 priorities, and they add time pressure to them so they don't slip through the calendar cracks. Here are some pro-tips you can use and pass onto your team for how to make calendar blocking work:

- Write the specific task you will complete during a given calendar block.
- Have a dedicated spot you go for Quadrant 2 tasks (for example a thinking chair).
- Turn off your notifications and hide from all interruptions.
- Schedule a silent coworking meeting with a co-conspirator for shared accountability.
- Schedule teamwide meeting-free days or blocks of time.

Another common *Quadrant* challenge we hear is that requests from leaders are often automatically perceived as Quadrant 1 tasks. Executives often tell us that they make a casual remark about a task only to discover later that it was interpreted as an order to stop everything else and focus on that task. As a leader in your organization, you can prevent this type of "deception" by **Deblurring** why and when something should be done. Be sure also to clarify the importance and urgency when you receive requests from other leaders. For example, "So that I know how to prioritize this, can you share how urgent it is and what it **Links up** to?" **Playback** or Split-track their reply to guarantee alignment.

Yet another frequent challenge managers and their teams come across when trying to stay true to their *Quadrant Method* insights is when one person's Quadrant 1 or 2 is another's Quadrant 3. This is very often the case, and the vocabulary of "urgent" and "important" becomes essential for negotiating priorities. Here is an example of an effective prioritization conversation between Olivia and Luca, keeping urgency and importance in mind:

Version 1: No Do-Over Needed!

Olivia: Hey, Luca. I noticed you still haven't replied to the email I sent two days ago asking for your input on the contract.

Luca: Yeah, sorry. I haven't been able to get around to it yet.

Olivia: I get it, but I bring it up because the vendor asked if we could get it back to them this week, <u>so it's now becoming urgent</u>. Would it be possible to prioritize?

Luca: I hate to slow you down, but here's my challenge: I'm working on a contract for our largest deal, <u>so it's important</u>, and I won't be able to get both done. Would it be possible to extend the deadline with the vendor by one week to reduce the urgency?

Prioritization Tool #3: Use the Bucket Method

For those who want to help their team combine time awareness and prioritization, we bring you the *Bucket Method*. This tool is as simple as it sounds but surprisingly effective. To put it to use, encourage your team members to pick their buckets of focus for the quarter. We strongly recommend no more than three buckets of focus at a time. You can also help bring greater clarity to the buckets by **Deblurring** what success looks like for each one. Every day, they can fill in the tasks they need to complete to make progress in each bucket. When stuck or overwhelmed, invite your team members to push the **Pause** button and ask, "Which bucket does this **Linkup** to?" or "What bucket am I working in right now?" For example:

1. Build app	2. Onboard new hires	3. Develop my team
Goal this quarter: add 3 new features	**Goal this quarter:** 4 weeks to proficiency	**Goal this quarter:** engagement score of 90%
Tasks for today: • Interview sales team to understand client needs	**Tasks for today:** • Create checklist for first week of onboarding	**Tasks for today:** • Give feedback to each team member • Announce shadowing program

Once you've helped your team members draw their buckets, get more out of this productivity tool faster by **Q-steps** with the following coaching questions and **Playing back** their replies:

- "What are your buckets for this quarter? What made you choose these?"
- "How do you define success for each one?"
- "What percentage of your time has been going to each bucket?"

- "What else have you been doing other than work in these three buckets? Does it make sense to adjust your buckets or find ways to reduce or eliminate the other activities?"
- "How can you push back on requests so it's possible to stick to your priorities?"

Often, the biggest source of help you can provide as a manager is to encourage your team members to say "no" to items that are not their *MITs*, Quadrant 1 or 2 tasks, or one of their buckets. Encourage them to ask prioritization questions of others like:

- "By when does this need to happen?"
- "Would it be possible to get this to you later than that time?"
- "Would you share what this **Links up** to so I can best prioritize?"

And ask prioritization questions of themselves, including:

- "Will I really add the most value today by doing X right now?"
- "Can I delegate this?"
- "Am I really adding value by perfecting this further or is it good enough?"

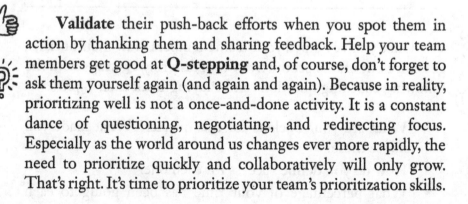

Validate their push-back efforts when you spot them in action by thanking them and sharing feedback. Help your team members get good at **Q-stepping** and, of course, don't forget to ask them yourself again (and again and again). Because in reality, prioritizing well is not a once-and-done activity. It is a constant dance of questioning, negotiating, and redirecting focus. Especially as the world around us changes ever more rapidly, the need to prioritize quickly and collaboratively will only grow. That's right. It's time to prioritize your team's prioritization skills.

Organization

In our research, we found that the most productive managers and teams we studied were also some of the most organized. They diligently tracked down and eliminated unnecessary aspects of their workflow. They delighted in finding new ways to increase their speed and efficiency. This is the essence of having organization skills. While prioritization is all about the why and the what, organization is about *how* you get things done. Even if you are not the type to have a perfectly organized sock drawer, or perhaps have no sock drawer at all, the two tools in this section will make it easier for you and your team to become more organized faster.

Organization Tool #1: Encourage a Consistent Capture System

Legend has it that Albert Einstein didn't know his own phone number or address. Why? He didn't want to waste valuable brain real estate with information that could be stored elsewhere. Even if you aren't perfecting a theory to explain space and time, you can get tremendous value from setting your and your team's minds free to solve problems, detect patterns, develop relationships, and generate new ideas.

By contrast, most people's minds are chock full of "open loops": swirling reminders and snippets of information. If you've ever found yourself tossing and turning in bed, hoping you'll remember to send that email or realizing you forgot an upcoming birthday, you've been the victim of a phenomenon known as the Zeigarnik effect. Psychologist Bluma Zeigarnik realized that people's minds tend to hold onto information and keep rehearsing it when a task is left unfinished (Zeigarnik 1938). This effect can be used for good. For example, the author Ernest Hemingway is said to have ended every writing day in the middle of a sentence so that his unconscious mind would keep working on the story. But the Zeigarnik effect contributes to stress, distractions, lost time, and cognitive lag when those open loops consist of information that can simply be recorded outside of one's mind (Masicampo and Baumeister 2011).

The solution? Encourage your team members to create a *Consistent Capture System (CCS)*, a concept inspired by author David Allen. A *CCS* is a reliable, go-to spot to record information instead of storing it in memory. The most important *CCS* types capture:

- To-do items
- Appointments and deadlines
- Notes (including key points, ideas, and instructions)

There are so many *CCS* tools available that at one point we decided to conduct a study to see if one tool outperforms another. We diligently compared the vast number of options we came across in our manager interviews and found . . . absolutely nothing. Some people use a digital solution, some use notebooks, some rely on sticky notes. The *CCS* itself didn't make a difference. What did matter was how *consistent* the *CCS* was. Folks who sometimes capture to-do items on their phones, sometimes on their calendars, and sometimes on a napkin they crumple up and promptly lose in the abyss of their backpacks have open loops because they can't trust their *CCS*. So encourage each team member to experiment with options, then pick one *CCS* that works best for their brains and **Pause** to capture their open loops as they appear. Be sure to keep yourself organized and model good organization habits by having a *CCS* of your own. For shared goals, projects, and information, co-create a consistent, transparent capture system with your team.

Organization Tool #2: Create a Closed Loop Culture

Once you and your team have a *CCS* in place, the next move to becoming organized faster is to create what we call a *Closed Loop Culture*. A *Closed Loop Culture* is a teamwide norm of noticing and helping to close open loops. Take a look at the following team conversation to see how a dedication to a *Closed Loop Culture* looks in practice:

Version 1: No Do-Over Needed!

Luca: Okay, so we've decided to proofread our existing materials to make sure there are no errors.

Olivia: Right. By when are you thinking we should get everything done?

Mia: I suggest we set a completion date of April 10. If a higher priority comes up, let's add it to the meeting agenda to discuss how best to prioritize.

Luca: That works for me. I'll capture it in our team calendar now.

Mia: Thank you. Before we move on, can we clarify who will be responsible for getting it done?

Kofi: I can drive the editing project. I'll email everyone by this Friday to clarify how each person can contribute. Does that work for everyone?

Luca: Thanks for offering to drive this. I'll add an action item for you right now in the meeting doc to get that message out to us by end of day this Friday.

Not only does a *Closed Loop Culture* enable shared accountability, but it also saves the entire team time and frustration trying to remember who was responsible for what and when. To

kick-start this norm on your team, model **Pausing** to ask **Deblurring** questions like, "who, what, when" questions, Play back what you hear, and use a shared *CCS* to capture the commitments people have made. Invite your team members to **Extract** open loops, ask open loop questions, **Play back** what they hear, and capture commitments.

Focus

How often would you guess your work gets interrupted? Interruption researcher Gloria Mark and her team followed around "knowledge workers" and discovered that they are typically interrupted every 12 minutes. That's bad enough as it is, but there's also a plot twist. Roughly 44% of these disruptions are "self-interruptions." In other words, we are our own focus enemies. A self-interruption is typically a sudden swerve from your workflow to check email, social media, the news, or the kitchen cabinet. The result? Interruptions increase stress, errors, frustration, and cognitive lag – leading to wasted time and worse performance (Mark, Gudith, and Klocke 2008). What's more, frequent interruptions mean less opportunity for flow state: a sense of total absorption that is one of the best predictors of work and life satisfaction (Csikszentmihalyi 2008). So what can you do to help yourself and your team become more focused faster? Squirrel! No really, here are three great tools to use and share.

Focus Tool #1: Co-create If-Thens

One lightweight solution to reduce internal and external distractions is to anticipate them in advance and create implementation intentions for how to handle them, or simply *if-thens*. Here's how *if-thens* work: designate any familiar cue in your environment as your "if," and use it to prompt any desired "then" behavior that will help you stay on track. Instead of deciding in

that moment how to handle a distraction, use your prepro-
grammed *if-then* to guide your actions. Help your team members come up with *if-thens* that eliminate their most common
distractions, and co-create *if-thens* as a team to support one
another's commitment to focus. Here are a few of our favorite
if-thens from our research:

Distraction	If	Then
Morning news/ social media	If I open my laptop –	Then I'll write my MITs.
Someone coming to you with a "quick" question	If someone asks a complicated question –	Then I'll ask to schedule time to discuss it.
Alerts and no-tifications	If I need to focus –	Then I will turn off all alerts.
New email	If it's 12 p.m. –	Then I'll batch-process email.
Frequent meetings	If it's Monday –	Then we have no meetings.
Shoulder taps from coworkers	If someone on our team has head-phones on –	Then we'll email them.
Instant messages from coworkers	If someone has their status set to "away" –	Then we won't message them until they're back.
Anything	If I/we complete this task –	Then I/we will get a point/high five/treat.

If-thens have been shown to increase the likelihood of a wide
range of behaviors, from changing eating and exercise habits to
doing timely health screenings (Gollwitzer and Sheeran 2006).
You might have even noticed that we provide several *if-then*
options in each chapter's Lab Report to help you put small leadership experiments into practice more quickly. To get started

using *if-thens*, co-create a list of common distractions with your team. Together, agree to an *if-then* you will all honor for at least one month. If this *if-then* becomes a habit, then consider adding more.

Focus Tool #2: Work in Pomodoros

A type of *if-then* that bloomed in popularity all around the world is a focus tool called the *Pomodoro Technique* (Italian for tomato). The tool's name comes from its creator, Francesco Cirillo, who used a tomato-shaped kitchen timer to stay focused on his work as a university student (Cirillo 2018). Here is how the *Pomodoro Technique* works:

- If the Pomodoro starts, then spend 25 minutes focused on a task.
- If 25 minutes pass, then take a mandatory 5-minute break.
- If you get interrupted (or interrupt yourself), then you have to start over.

You can encourage your team to spend their entire day working in Pomodoros or reserve it for tasks that require an extra degree of focus. The managers we interviewed reported that their teams used Pomodoros for everything from email to research to planning to hashing out conflict. It is also a terrific tool to overcome procrastination. Just put in one "Pomodoro's worth" of focus as a way to rapidly kick-start motivation. Pitch the Pomodoro as a technique to your team members, use it yourself, and co-work in *Pomodoros* as a way to create shared accountability.

Focus Tool #3: Use the Kanban System

The final productivity tool we'll share is great for helping your team improve focus, and can also improve time awareness, prior-itization, and organization. This multifaceted tool is called the *Kanban System*. Kanban is the Japanese word for "sign," popular-ized by Toyota car manufacturing where managers introduced visual signs to increase production efficiency. A classic Kanban board looks like this:

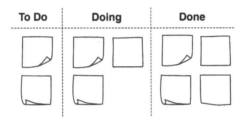

Source: LifeLabs Learning.

Each to-do item is represented on a card. Cards start their journey in the Backlog or To Do column (a *CCS*). Once you are ready to begin working on a task, you physically (or digitally) move that card to the Doing column. This simple action is at the heart of the *Kanban System's* ability to generate focus. It is a meaningful **Pause** and an explicit agreement between you and your brain about the task you will be working on until you are ready to move it into the glorious Done column. Bonus: if you jot down how long the task took you, your Done column can moonlight as a *time audit* . . . making it easy to **Extract** insights about your work. Many of the great managers we studied had some version of a team *Kanban* board – whether it was a white-board or a digital tool. Several also used a personal *Kanban* board and encouraged their team members to use a *Kanban System* as their *CCS*. If you're not sure which tool to use first, this is a great one to pick since it packs such a powerful productivity punch.

Practice Station

Before we wrap up, let's return to the beginning. Has your productivity diagnosis of your team members changed since the start of this chapter? What do you see as each person's biggest area for improvement: time awareness, prioritization, organization, or focus? Remember that picking just one area of focus will help your team become more productive faster. Next, choose one tool from this chapter and share it with each person.

***

In summary: Accelerate your team's productivity by **Q-stepping** to diagnose each person's biggest challenge: time awareness, prioritization, organization, or focus. Suggest trying one productivity tool at a time from that category: *time language, start/stop on time, time audit, MITs, Quadrants, Buckets, CCS, Closed Loop Culture, If-thens, Pomodoro, Kanban.* Develop a habit of **Pausing** to slow down and consider whether your team is using time well.

Keep in mind that productivity isn't just a measure of high performance – it is what makes the difference between the days that leave your team members feeling exhausted but empty and the days they know they've made a difference. Just as financial skills help you get the most out of your money, productivity skills help you and your team transform time into the kind of progress that makes work matter.

MY LAB REPORT	Today's Date:
My takeaways:	
I regularly help my team make the best use of their time:	1 2 3 4 5 6 7 8 9 10 (strongly disagree) (strongly agree)
Experiment idea bank:	• If I'm speaking about time, then I will use precise (blur-word-free) language. • If we have a team meeting, then I will ask everyone to share their MITs. • If someone commits to doing something, then I will ask, "Where shall we capture that?"
One small experiment I'll try to increase my score by 1 point:	
Post-experiment Learning Extractions:	

Bonus: Want to take your manager skills to the next level? Check out the bonus Inclusion Stations at leaderlab.lifelabs-learning.com.

My Learning Tracker

7 out of 7 Core BUs collected. 3 of 8 Core Skills collected.

Q-step	Playback	Deblur	Validate	Linkup	Pause	Extract
Coaching	Feedback	Productivity				

11

Effective One-on-Ones

Imagine you are halfway through your workday and feeling unproductive. Somehow your to-do list has only grown since the morning. You glance at your calendar and notice that you have a one-on-one coming up with a team member. There's nothing urgent to discuss, and you just met yesterday to give input on their work. Your cursor hovers over the cancel button. Should you hit it? Based on our research, the answer is *no*. By the end of this chapter, we hope you will agree and go into your next one-on-one more confident about how to put this time to great use.

Why dedicate an entire chapter to leading *effective one-on-ones*? So far, we've shared three tipping point skills that differentiate great managers from average: coaching, feedback, and productivity. These skills are the "how." But rarely is a "how" useful without a "where." To put these skills into practice, the highest leverage "where" is the humble one-on-one. While it seems like a meager 30- or 60-minute calendar block, consistent one-on-ones are a manager's single greatest resource. For these meetings to be effective, they have to be frequent. In fact, monthly one-on-ones actually lead to less engagement than having no one-on-ones at all (Clifton and Harter 2019). And regularly scheduled one-on-ones predict better engagement and performance (Mann and Darby 2014). How does the one-on-one do all this? Here are the top three reasons:

1. **Trust via the mere-exposure effect:** Simply seeing one another's faces leads to greater trust and liking, a phenomenon known as the mere-exposure effect, coined by psychologist Robert Zajonc (1968). In one fascinating study, researchers found that people rated individuals they had seen before – even without interacting – 15% more positively than total strangers (Moreland and Beach 1992). More trust leads to more open communication, allowing obstacles to be removed swiftly and catalyzing more courage to explore and experiment.

2. **Accountability via progress reporting:** Beyond mere exposure, meeting frequently creates a culture of accountability. The one-on-one becomes a checkpoint to celebrate progress

and overcome obstacles. Not only does this practice increase productivity, but it also drives engagement. Research shows that when employees believe their manager doesn't hold them accountable, a whopping 69% are actively disengaged and only 3% report being engaged (Mann and Darby 2014).

3. **Agility via short feedback loops:** A weekly cadence allows for accelerated learning. The more frequently you can give feedback and **Pause** to **Extract** learnings, the more quickly you can **Deblur** expectations and help improve performance. In an ever-changing environment, every week also brings new challenges and opportunities. A weekly touchpoint also lets managers coach, swiftly adjust priorities, and address any engagement and productivity challenges that pop up.

So, it's clear that one-on-ones are important. But how exactly do you fill that time other than just staring at people and waiting for the mere-exposure effect to kick in? Effective one-on-ones begin with the recognition that the most important direct outcome of these conversations is increased engagement. Engagement is a heightened emotional connection to work that drives people to make greater contributions.

Practice Station

Pause for a moment and think about your own engagement history. Think of times you have been disengaged. What was the result? How about times your engagement levels surged? What was the impact?

The most engaged teams (comparing the top quartile to the bottom quartile) have (Clifton and Harter 2019):

- 20% higher sales
- 21% higher profitability
- 40% fewer quality defects
- 41% lower absenteeism
- 24% less turnover (in high-turnover companies)
- 59% less turnover (in low-turnover companies)

While there are many things companies can do on a systems level to increase engagement, individual needs are, well, individual. Managers have the very best opportunity to monitor and help increase each person's engagement levels based on their unique needs. This is an essential aspect of the manager job description. With each dip in engagement, the entire team's productivity suffers.

Engagement and disengagement are also contagious. Have you ever worked with someone who hated their job? It's as though the cloud hanging over their heads stretches out to eclipse everyone else's sunshine too. It works the other way around too. Engaged people make others more engaged and more productive. In one study, researchers found that just sitting close to someone highly productive (or unproductive) impacted their neighbors' productivity (Corsello and Minor 2017).

So how can you use one-on-ones to monitor and help increase each team member's engagement? First, let's touch on what *not* to do. In our research, we saw that average managers turned their one-on-one conversations into status updates and "quick questions" that could have been handled more efficiently via email, spreadsheets, team meetings, or a Kanban board (see Chapter 10). Instead, great managers look at every one-on-one through the lens of the biggest drivers of engagement.

What drives engagement? Based on years of research kick-started by psychologists Richard Ryan and Edward Deci, we know that when five specific "brain cravings" are satisfied, the result is engagement. Knowing these brain cravings simplifies complexity and helps you become a great manager faster. What are they? Certainty, Autonomy, Meaning, Progress, and Social inclusion (including belonging and connection). To help you easily remember these brain cravings in the midst of each one-on-one, we bring you the LifeLabs Learning *CAMPS Model*:

- Certainty
- Autonomy
- Meaning
- Progress
- Social inclusion

To embed this framework into your memory, think about your team's engagement falling into one of two *CAMPS*: engaged versus disengaged.

In the rest of this chapter, we'll look at each brain craving one at a time, both in terms of how to apply each one to the *structure* of your one-on-ones and in terms of the *content* of your one-on-one conversations. By structure, we mean the actual agenda template that you use for your one-on-one meetings. While many managers don't use a template at all and opt for the "go with the flow" strategy, we've found that most great managers use a template to keep important conversations from slipping through the cracks. Throughout this chapter, we'll share structure recommendations and a sample agenda template at the end. Show the template to each member of your team, and tweak it together to prompt the conversations you most value.

Brain Craving #1: Certainty

One of the biggest cravings our brains have is for *certainty*. Most people don't do well with too much uncertainty, especially when the stakes are high. Uncertainty triggers the sympathetic nervous system to release the stress hormone cortisol, causing a fight-or-flight state rather than the curiosity and connection states that lead to success at work (Peters, McEwen, and Friston 2017). Aside from the psychological burden of having too many unknowns, uncertainty can also cause logistical bottlenecks. When employees don't know what's expected of them, what to prioritize, or how success is defined, they waste countless hours searching for answers, making poor decisions, or just waiting around until someone comes along with the information.

How to Add Certainty to Your One-on-One Structure

You can begin to feed people's brain craving for certainty with the structure of the one-on-one itself. Here are a few of our favorite certainty-building tactics:

- **Consistency:** Schedule your one-on-ones to be the same time and day of the week every week. Avoid canceling. While it might seem like the right thing to do during a week full of *Quadrant* 1 action (see Chapter 10), a canceled one-on-one sends a signal to your team members that their time and needs aren't important.
- **Template:** Co-create a conversation template (see the sample at the end of this chapter) and ask your team members to come to each one-on-one meeting with the agenda filled out. In this way, they'll know what to discuss, and you'll make the best use of time.

- **Ritual:** Build in an element of ritual into the one-one-one as an opportunity to **Pause** together. For example, many of the managers we studied had a start and/or stop ritual in their one-on-ones, like **Extracting** the learning from the prior week in the first five minutes or ending with a "stretch question" to bring the conversation in a new direction each time. Creating certainty doesn't mean eliminating variety.

How to Diagnose and Increase Certainty Through Your One-on-One Conversations

Aside from weaving certainty into the fabric of the one-on-one structure, you can also use your one-on-one time to diagnose your team members' level of certainty and proactively increase it. How can you spot certainty gaps through your one-on-ones? Keep an eye out for signs of confusion, insecurity, threat, and an overwhelmed state. Take a look at the conversation below to see a classic example of an uncertainty overdose:

Version 1

Mia: How has your week been?

Luca: Not good, honestly. My head has been spinning.

Mia: What's on your mind?

Luca: I just can't focus on any one task. Every time I start something, I wonder if I should be doing something else. I'm not even sure what we're trying to achieve with the project this quarter and how we'll get everything done by the deadline. I want to delegate some of my work to Kofi, but honestly, I just start questioning what my job will even be if I give my work away.

> **Mia:** Yikes. That sounds overwhelming. Is there anything else on your mind?
>
> **Luca:** Actually, yeah. A lot of the work we're trying to do has to do with better analytics, but we don't have the software to be able to track these numbers automatically. Plus there's the possible merger looming on the horizon. I have no idea how that will impact any of us.
>
> **Mia:** Yeah, that's keeping me up at night too.

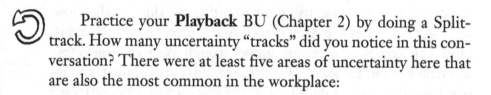

Practice your **Playback** BU (Chapter 2) by doing a Split-track. How many uncertainty "tracks" did you notice in this conversation? There were at least five areas of uncertainty here that are also the most common in the workplace:

1. Goals
2. Roles
3. Priorities
4. Resources
5. Overall job security

Your one-on-ones are an excellent time to fill these certainty gaps whenever you notice them. If you believe that your team members already have the information they need, coach them to figure things out on their own. These uncertainty signals can also be your cue to either **Deblur** or provide more information (tell versus ask). Mia realizes this after her one-on-one with Luca, so she hits the Do-Over Button to go back and add more certainty where she can:

Version 2: Do-Over

Mia: Okay, so if I'm hearing you right, it sounds like there are a few things that feel uncertain: our goal, your role, priorities, resources, and the possible merger. Is that right?

Luca: Yes. I think that's everything. No wonder my head is spinning.

Mia: Yeah, it's a lot. <u>Let's figure these out one by one.</u> Where do we start?

Luca: To be honest, it's tough to think about anything clearly in the midst of all the merger rumors. I just don't know what to expect.

Mia: <u>How about separating it out into things you can control and things you can't control?</u>

Luca: Okay, well . . . if the merger happens, I *can't* control which roles they choose to keep and cut. That part is scary. But there's nothing I can do about it. What I *can* control is doing great work so if there's a new leadership team, they see me and our team as important contributors. I guess that's part of the thing that's stressing me out. I don't even know if I'm doing a good job these days.

Mia: That's a good insight: what you *can* control is the quality of your work. <u>Getting aligned on the other areas you mentioned – goals, roles, priorities, resources – will make that possible. Right?</u>

Luca: Right. So, can we talk about the goal? I know what we're supposed to do but not really how we're measuring success, which makes it hard to make decisions.

> **Mia:** Yes, good point. That's on me. I should have **deblurred** the goal. <u>The metric we're working toward is cutting production time by 20%</u>. With that in mind, which of your tasks strike you as most urgent and important?

Whenever you spot those red flags signaling a lack of certainty, **Q-step** or supply missing information. You can also assess and improve certainty levels proactively. This is especially good to do during role transitions, priority changes, and team or company changes. Below are just a few certainty-related coaching questions you can ask in your one-on-ones. For even greater shared certainty, **Play back** what you hear:

Sample Certainty Questions

- On a scale of 1–10, how satisfied are you with how much certainty you have at work?
- What does success look like to you?
- What do you wish you felt more secure or clear about at work?
- What resources or information are missing or hard to access?
- Let's make sure we're aligned. What do you see as your top priorities?
- Where might it help you to have more routines or rituals?

(For each question, you can follow up with: What would increase your score by one point?)

In a rapidly changing environment, achieving complete certainty is an unrealistic goal. And too much certainty can even lead to boredom. In one shocking study, researchers found that when given a choice of being bored or applying a painful electric current to their skin, most people chose the electric shock (Wilson et al. 2014). Besides, every person on your team will have a different degree of comfort and skill in navigating uncertainty. The job of a manager is not to hunt down and eradicate all unknowns. Instead, the goal is to help shine a light on the gaps, then work together to close as many of those gaps as feasible. Even in the absence of certain answers, you can provide certainty of communication. For example, during the chaos of the 2020 pandemic and recession, some of the best leaders we studied created a predictable cadence of updates, sharing company news even if the news was "there is no news."

Brain Craving #2: Autonomy

Work is often stressful, so on the surface, it would seem that the work of entrepreneurs is the most stressful of all. If you are launching a business, there is boundless unpredictability, endless responsibility, and few people to turn to for help. You'd think that the payoff would be higher earnings, but the truth is that most entrepreneurs make less money than full-time, salaried employees (Hamilton 2000). So entrepreneurs earn less, work more, and face relentless uncertainty. And yet people who work for themselves tend to have greater job satisfaction (Blanchflower 2000). How could this be? It turns out that autonomy is a buffer for stress. When you have the right amount of choice and control, negative stress turns to eustress – that buzzy, feel-good sensation you get when you are enjoying a challenge.

It's also true that when you have too much autonomy, uncertainty and anxiety kick in. So, the goal is balance. Throwing someone into the deep end when they don't know how to swim is too much autonomy. Sitting on their back and paddling their arms for them is not enough autonomy. Think about times you felt that someone was paddling your arms for you. Perhaps you had a micromanager or even an overly controlling parent. How did it feel? When we ask our workshop participants, the most common answers we get are "soul-crushing," "agonizing," "deflating," "draining," and "demotivating" – all pretty terrible sensations.

Having the right amount of autonomy at work leads to more engagement, commitment, and productivity (Slemp et al. 2018). Average managers we studied – particularly managers who led remotely – often toggled between too much and too little autonomy. Great managers put in the effort to find the right balance. The one-on-one is the perfect place to learn from each person on your team whether they have too little, too much, or just the right level of autonomy.

How to Add Autonomy to Your One-on-One Structure

- **Ownership: Deblur** the ownership of these meetings. Clarify that one-on-ones are your team members' meetings (not yours). For example, "These one-on-ones are here for you to get the support you need. So please add what's most helpful to you onto the agenda." When you notice them starting to add their own items to the agenda, **Validate** their efforts by sharing feedback and encouragement.

- **Choice:** Ask each team member to decide when and where you'll meet. Encourage them to pick a time they find most convenient and brain-friendly. If you have location options, give them their choice of office, cafe, park, video platform, and so on.

How to Diagnose and Increase Autonomy Satisfaction in Your One-on-Ones

You can spot too much autonomy in the same ways as too much uncertainty. Team members drowning in autonomy will come across as worried, cautious, and indecisive. In these cases, your job is to coach and provide missing information. When in doubt, **Q-step** with, "How can I be most helpful: would you rather get advice or would it be useful if I asked questions to help think through this?"

Diagnosing a state of too little autonomy can be trickier unless someone tells you directly what they're experiencing. Take a look at the following interaction between Mia and Kofi, and see if you notice the symptoms:

Version 1

Mia: Hey, Kofi. Is now a good time to talk about the proofreading project you're driving?

Kofi: Yeah, sure.

Mia: Great. You said you'd create a shared document for all our materials so we can edit them at the same time. I noticed you haven't made it yet, and I mention it because it means clients are still receiving materials with typos, which makes us look unprofessional. What got in your way?

Kofi: I'm sorry. I guess I just forgot.

Mia: Okay . . . I think creating a shared doc is the best next step. Do you see it that way too?

Kofi: Yeah, I can do it your way if that's what everyone wants.

Mia: Okay. Well, thanks.

Kofi is showing two tell-tale signs of having too little autonomy. Did you notice them? The most common sign is a lack of follow-through. Someone might agree to do something, then drop the ball. Sometimes this happens on purpose, and sometimes it's simply the result of forgetting information that doesn't interest us. The other common sign of too little autonomy is what can be described as disengaged compliance. It's a "yeah, whatever" approach that people sometimes adopt as a coping mechanism. In this state, people follow instructions, but they put in little or no personal care, effort, or creativity.

At first, Mia is taken aback by Kofi's behavior. During the first few months in the role, he was so eager for guidance. Now that he is becoming increasingly confident, she didn't notice that he started craving more autonomy. What can you do once you spot similar symptoms? See how Mia handles the situation once she hits her Do-Over Button:

Version 2: Do-Over

Mia: I think creating a shared doc is the best next step. Do you see it that way too?

Kofi: Yeah, I can do it your way if that's what everyone wants.

Mia: Hey, Kofi, can we actually pause for a moment? <u>I might be wrong here, but it seems like you disagree with this approach but feel like you have to do it anyway. Is that right</u>?

Kofi: I mean . . . I already shared my concerns several times, and everyone just talks over each other. There's no point in continuing to bring it up. I'll just do what you all decided. I'm too new here to make a fuss, anyway. You all have your way of doing things.

Mia: That must be frustrating. <u>I want you to have a say. We're all one team now, and we wanted you to join because we all thought we could benefit from your</u>

> perspective. I'm curious, <u>is it just this project or are</u>
> <u>there also other areas at work where you don't have</u>
> <u>a good amount of autonomy?</u>
>
> **Kofi:** Well . . . to be honest, this project is minor. I don't
> think it would bother me, but what's been frustrating
> lately is that there are so many rules in place. I guess
> I was just hoping to be on a team where we can trust
> each other to make judgment calls. Since I'm exceed-
> ing my targets now, I was hoping to have more crea-
> tive freedom.

Thanks to some artful **Q-steps**, **Playbacks**, and **Validation**, Mia knows that Kofi is missing a sense of *voice* and *choice* – the two biggest aspects of autonomy (which luckily rhyme, making them easier to recall).

How can you give people more voice? Pull for feedback and input early and often. This can be a formal process or as simple as saying, "I'm planning to do this thing. Can I hear your thoughts on it before I make a final decision?" If you don't end up applying the ideas people contribute, **Link up** to explain the reasoning. You can also hold ritualized retrospectives to **Extract** learning together and generate ideas for how to apply lessons from the past in the future.

How can you give people choice? Offer options in tasks, projects, and responsibilities whenever it's possible to do so. You can also offer autonomy around *how* to do the work. Coaching (see Chapter 8) is an excellent autonomy tool because it helps people come to their own conclusions about how to solve a prob-lem, even if that problem was assigned to them. It is also ideal to invite people to set their own goals or at least to develop them collaboratively. Research shows that employees whose managers help them set their own performance goals are 170% more likely to be engaged (Mann and Darby 2014).

In instances where little or no autonomy is possible in the work itself, get creative with "peripheral autonomy" you might offer options such as where and when to do the work. One manager we studied supervised a motorcycle manufacturing process with little room for creative freedom (there are only so many ways to correctly assemble a motorcycle). To create a sense of choice, he made a point of letting people pick music to play through the factory speakers, plan team celebrations, co-create meeting agendas, and choose their shifts.

Another excellent autonomy-building strategy that combines voice and choice is giving people *ownership* over at least one area of work that is meaningful to them. To own a responsibility or outcome means to be fully accountable for its success or failure. It means having decision-making power and access to the resources needed to achieve the necessary result. Whenever you notice signs of too much or too little autonomy, use your one-on-ones to investigate the cause. Following are sample questions you can ask:

Sample Autonomy Questions

- On a scale of 1–10, how satisfied are you with how much autonomy you have at work?
- Where do you wish you had more (or less) choice?
- How happy are you with how often you are in charge of your work?
- What are areas in which you wish you had either more freedom or more direction?

- Do you feel a bit micromanaged in any areas? What do you think is causing it?
- What are some areas where you'd like your voice to be heard more?

(For each question, you can follow up with: What would increase your score by one point?)

Brain Craving #3: Meaning

When psychologist Viktor Frankl was held captive in a Nazi concentration camp during the Holocaust, he experienced first-hand what happens when people are exposed to chronic stress, fear, and anxiety. Observing the effects of this environment, he came to a surprising conclusion. The most dangerous thing that can happen to us from a psychological perspective is not the stress of the situation, but a loss of meaning. Frankl referred to this state as an "existential vacuum," and he believed that, even in our typical daily lives, it is our biggest barrier to resilience, engagement, and fulfillment (1946). Many years later, the research continues to support his hypothesis. When you help employees connect work to concepts that matter to them, it increases their engagement, satisfaction, and productivity (Berg, Dutton, and Wrzesniewski 2013). The **Linkup** to meaning can be as simple as remembering what's in it for us, but often, the even more energizing fuel is seeing the positive impact you are making on others.

How to Add Meaning to Your One-on-One Structure

- **Purpose:** A simple way to make your one-on-ones more meaningful is to **Link up** to why one-on-ones matter in the first place. This is a great practice when you are new to working together or if you've never set expectations about the purpose of these meetings. For example, "These one-on-ones are your time to bring up anything that will help you be even more engaged and productive and to keep investing in your growth."

- **Focus:** You can also **Link up** to the purpose of one-on-ones whenever you notice the focus of your conversations turning into status updates or information sessions. Suggest using a different forum for these topics or time-boxing them so there is space left over to make progress on their challenges, goals, and personal development.

How to Diagnose and Increase Meaning in Your One-on-Ones

How can you tell that someone on your team is trapped within an existential vacuum – even if it's just one of those little hand-held vacuums? A common sign of meaninglessness at work is burnout: fatigue, alienation from others, cynicism, mistakes, and absenteeism. Though most people associate burnout with the exhaustion that creeps in when they are overworked, one of the biggest predictors of burnout is actually a loss of meaning. See if you can spot it in this exchange with Mia and Olivia:

Version 1

Mia:	How has your week been so far?
Olivia:	Fine, I guess.
Mia:	. . . Okay. What was a highlight for you?
Olivia:	Uh . . . nothing really. All the days have kind of been blurring together. I'm just tired.
Mia:	That's not fun. Want to talk about it?
Olivia:	If you want.

Of course, meaning won't solve all the causes of burnout and disengagement, but increasing meaning is at least partially within a manager's scope of control (and responsibility), so it's a worthwhile brain craving to prioritize. How can you engineer a greater sense of meaning for your team members? The simplest solution is to think of your brain as a linking machine. Whenever you take an action, your brain "reaches out" to find the **Linkup** to the reason for that action. Without even realizing it, you ask, "Why am I doing this?" and "Is it worth it?" When you can't find a good reason, that existential vacuum starts to suck at your soul. On the other hand, when the answers to these questions **Link up** to your personal values, even seemingly menial tasks can flood you with motivation.

Use your one-on-ones to create a stronger **Linkup** to the things that matter to each person on your team. Ask about their values, what energizes them, and what results they find most meaningful. Any signs of excitement and fulfillment are great opportunities to learn by **Q-stepping** with questions like "What was important to you about that?" "What was the best part?" or "What was it about this situation that felt so good?" and **Playing back** the key points.

Then, whenever you give feedback and progress updates, **Link up** to the things each person finds meaningful by sharing a personalized impact statement (from Chapter 9). You can deliver feedback directly from your perspective, pass on praise from others, and – when possible – give people direct access to observe the impact they're making. As a manager, finding creative ways to show people their impact is a terrific use of your time. The impact is substantial. For example, radiologists who saw photos of their patients improved the accuracy of their diagnoses by 46% (Turner and Hadas-Halpern 2008). And call center employees who heard a five-minute talk by a student benefiting from a scholarship they helped raise funds for increased the amount of money they raised by 171% (Grant et al. 2007). Keeping the importance of meaning in mind, Mia decides to hit the magic Do-Over Button and try the conversation with Olivia once more:

Version 2: Do-Over

Mia: How has your week been so far?

Olivia: Fine.

Mia: What was a highlight for you?

Olivia: Uh . . . nothing really. All the days have kind of been blurring together. I'm just tired.

Mia: That's tough. <u>When was the last time you felt energized by your work</u>?

Olivia: Ugh . . . Probably last year's conference. I remember being on such a high after that. I haven't felt that in a long time.

Mia: <u>What do you think it was about that conference that was motivating</u>?

Olivia: I guess just seeing how all these companies were able to benefit from our work.

Mia: <u>What's important to you about that</u>?

Olivia: Well, at the end of the day, I want to help people make better decisions. It was exciting to see how our analytics make that possible. But usually, I have no idea how people use the data we present once we send it to them.

Mia: <u>Sounds like you'd like more visibility into how clients are using the data</u>.

Olivia: Yeah, that would be good.

Mia: That makes sense. I think we can all benefit from that. <u>How do you think we can get access to that information on a regular basis</u>?

> **Olivia:** Hm. Well, one thing I can do is create an auto-
> mated message that goes out after like three
> months asking clients how things are going. Or
> maybe we can even do a quarterly case study!

While there may be no quick solution to Olivia's dip in
meaning, notice how her engagement starts to climb thanks to
 Mia's **Validation** statements and by starting to generate some
ideas. Research shows that searching for small ways to make
work more meaningful results in greater engagement and performance (Rudolph et al. 2017). If you detect early signs of burnout or disengagement, or if you haven't checked in on meaning
in a while, here are some of our favorite questions to ask in
one-on-ones:

Sample Meaning Questions

- On a scale of 1–10, how satisfied are you with how
  much meaning you have at work?
- What matters to you about ____?
- What's a recent contribution you are proud of?
- Where would you like to make more of an impact?
- How satisfied are you with how much recognition
  you get for your work?
- What are you looking forward to?

(For each question, you can follow up with: What
would increase your score by one point?)

Brain Craving #4: Progress

Take a moment to reflect on your work. What gives you the biggest spikes in engagement? If you're really curious, you can start keeping track. Or, if you prefer a more efficient answer, consider the research already conducted by Teresa Amabile and her team (2011), where they asked participants to do just that. Employees tracked all their activities and rated how satisfied they were each day. What differentiated the good days from the bad ones and the meh ones? In 76% of all good days, people mentioned experiencing a sense of progress. The most surprising finding from this research was that small, steady bursts of progress beat out big but infrequent wins. When it comes to engagement, it's not the major wins that matter most but a sense of steady achievement. Neurologically, when we hit or even anticipate hitting our goals, we experience a burst of dopamine – that addicting neurotransmitter that sends a reward signal to our brains. It creates a virtuous cycle with progress triggering dopamine, leading to more engagement, which fuels more progress, which leads to more dopamine, which leads to more engagement. So as a manager, how can you be a dope (that is, dopamine) dealer for your team?

How to Add Progress to Your One-on-One Structure

- **Goals:** Turn your one-on-one agenda into a dopamine doc. Either link to a *CCS* or use the one-on-one document to track goals and mark each one when it is accomplished. This practice lets you **Deblur** goals, creates accountability, and doubles as a development tracker you can review together to celebrate how far each person has come.
- **Small wins:** Start each one-on-one by asking each person to call out what went well. This ritual also creates a sense of certainty. Plus, learning why each win matters shows you

what gives each person a sense of meaning. But even more than that, regularly **Pausing** to demarcate wins gives your team more bang for each progress buck they earn. When they know they'll be sharing wins weekly, they'll keep an eye out for them – getting that dopamine hit when wins happen *and again* in the one-on-one conversation. When we spoke to the team members of John, one of the great managers we interviewed, several people confessed that his dedication to acknowledging wins trickled into their parenting. One person even started all dinners by sharing wins. They said they became better parents and closer families as a result.

- **Individual development:** Add a prompt to your one-on-one template to check in on individual development. This can serve as an opportunity to give feedback and a nudge to stay on track with building a new skill or knowledge area (more on this in Chapter 15).

How to Diagnose and Increase Progress in Your One-on-Ones

How do you know someone's dopamine levels are droopy? One of the most deceptive symptoms of low dopamine is chronic busyness. When your team members are pulled in multiple directions, have unclear priorities, or don't build in time to **Pause** and **Extract** their learnings, they end each week feeling less accomplished than when they started. This is a frustrating and demoralizing trap that's important to help your team members avoid. Here's how:

First, be sure to turn roadblocks into coaching opportunities. Remember the coaching moments to look out for (from Chapter 8)? Conundrums, Complaints, and Confidence issues are all red flags signaling problems with progress. Whenever team members bring these up, use them as an opportunity to **Q-step** and take the *SOON Funnel* out for a spin.

When people are procrastinating, a great progress-building practice is task-boxing. Procrastination is almost always a cue that someone isn't clear about all of the work involved in an assignment. Task-boxing means articulating, **Deblurring**, and visualizing each component of a task. For example, you might say: "Let's work backwards. Write out all the parts of the project starting with the end. What is the last part? What milestone would you have to hit before that? How about before that? What's the smallest step you can take to get started?"

Sample Task Box: Write a Blog Post					
1. Create outline	2. Ask for feedback	3. Write draft	4. Edit it	5. Select photo	6. Publish post

And to create a feeling of personal progress rather than simply task-based progress, be sure to also make time in your on-on-ones to for individual development. While feedback on work is essential, it might not be immediately clear how work progress builds skills and knowledge that transfer to create overall career progress. As a manager, you have the opportunity to **Extract** and demarcate your team members' growth simply by calling it out. Look at how Mia does it in the following conversation:

Version 1: No Do-Over Needed!
Luca: Thanks for the chat last week, Mia. I'm finally making decent progress on my to-do list again and the analytics project.

Mia: That's great. I know you've also been eager to develop new skills and had originally thought this initiative can be an opportunity to build your project management skills. Is that still the case?

Luca: Well, I guess I haven't been thinking about it that way. I've just been too busy.

Mia: I get that. From my perspective though, it looks like you already are developing your project management skills. Would it be helpful if I shared my feedback about it?

Luca: Yeah, please.

Mia: I noticed that in our last conversation, you pointed out we're missing software to automate our work. I mention it because that insight will help us achieve our goals faster. I see identifying obstacles and proposing solutions as a key aspect of project management skills. What do you think?

Luca: Yeah, I guess that's true. Thanks for pointing that out.

Whenever you spot a development milestone (like a completed assignment or achieved goal) demarcate it. This is the fourth C of the *4C* coaching moments: Completion. We'll delve much deeper into people development skills in Chapter 15. In the meanwhile, here are some simple but powerful questions you can ask in your one-on-ones to get the progress party started:

Sample Progress Questions

- On a scale of 1–10, how satisfied are you with how much progress you make at work?
- Where do you wish you felt more progress?

- What (or who) is blocking you or getting in your way of making progress?

- How often do you get a sense of uninterrupted flow at work?

- How satisfied are you with your sense of growth and learning?

- What were your wins this past week, and what learning can you **Extract** from them?

(For each question, you can follow up with: What would increase your score by one point?)

Brain Craving #5: Social Inclusion

Think of a time you felt excluded or like you didn't belong. Concentrate on that sensation for a moment. Neuropsychologists have discovered something fascinating about exclusion. In a study by Naomi Eisenberger and team, participants climbed inside an fMRI machine while playing a simple computer game in which they tossed a ball back and forth with two other participants (Eisenberger, Liebermann, and Williams 2003). All was well and good with the game until suddenly, two players started lobbing the ball back and forth to each other, totally leaving out one participant.

As you might have guessed, the game was rigged by the sneaky researchers. The other two players were computer-operated, but the (human) participants had no idea. Then again, why would they care? These were strangers. It also wasn't a particularly riveting game. But the participants' brains reacted as though this was a very big deal. It turns out our neural pathways for the pain of exclusion map onto the neural pathways for *physical pain.* Research shows that being excluded is so similar to being physically hurt that taking Tylenol can actually reduce emotional pain (Dewall et al. 2010). In short: being left out hurts. That sting of being underappreciated, left out, or – worst of all – forgotten cuts straight to the core, immediately reducing engagement and productivity. Researchers in the field of epigenetics have even discovered that social isolation can reduce immune system function, making people more vulnerable to disease (Cole et al. 2015).

We all need social inclusion. In the workplace, the absence of it hurts, and the presence of it improves commitment, time-to-performance, resilience, and employee retention. Yet it's so easy to brush off this need or take it for granted. One manager we studied told us about her vivid memory learning about the importance of social inclusion at work. She had three team members who all sat side by side in a cramped office. Then, to everyone's delight, the company leased another floor, making it possible for employees to spread out. The next day, the manager came into the office to find her typically calm and collected team member in tears. Their two other coworkers had decided to move to the new office floor, leaving the third person feeling utterly rejected. There was no malice in the move, but it took several days of dialogue to rebuild team cohesion and productivity.

But there's more to the social inclusion story than just being invited. While we all harbor the need to belong, we also need to retain our sense of individuality. That balance of being one of the group while still distinct from the group is a concept named *Optimal Distinctiveness* by psychologist Marilynn Brewer (1991). Achieving this ideal point pays off. For example, in a study of a large call center, researchers found that employees who received sweatshirts with the company logo *and* their name along with an opportunity to share their "best selves" had 250% lower attrition rates than employees who received swag with only the company name and onboarding focused only on the company (Cable, Gino, and Staats 2013). Great managers are always on the lookout for how to help each member of their team achieve that Optimal Distinctiveness balance. As Marta, one of the great managers interviewed, told us: "In every one-on-one, my goal is to help people feel like they can show up as their real selves – flaws, quirks and all. That's what makes it possible for them and us as a team to become the best version of ourselves." Here's how to make that happen:

How to Build Social Inclusion Through Your One-on-One Structure

- **Small talk:** We have been advocating for a structured one-on-one format throughout this chapter, and yet we also encourage space in every conversation for what linguists call "phatic communication" – unstructured interactions that signal care and interest. At LifeLabs Learning, we refer to this habit as "checking *in* before checking *on*." Most people refer to this type of communication as small talk, but there is nothing small about it. More small talk leads to more trust and greater team cohesion (Coupland 2003). Research also shows that meetings that begin with small talk are more effective (Allen, Lehmann-Willenbrock, and Landowski 2014). The primate equivalent of phatic communication is grooming. Research shows that the more time primates spend grooming one another, the closer their bond and the more likely they are to risk their lives for one another (Schino 2007). We humans have a lot to learn from the monkeys.

- **Body language:** Aside from the words you exchange in each one-on-one, pay close attention to your nonverbal communication. For example, turn toward the person you're meeting with, lean in, and uncross your arms to signal interest. Even when meeting virtually, body language can speak volumes. Encourage having cameras on, and set up your screen so that it is at your eye level rather than towering over someone (also known as the giant nostril frame), staring up at them, or looking to the side.

How to Diagnose and Increase Social Inclusion in Your One-on-Ones

Unless you have an fMRI machine lying around at work, it might be hard to know when someone on your team is lacking social inclusion. Some people cope with that lack of connection by disengaging and keeping to themselves. Others show up to every social function or demand to be included in more meetings. If you work in-person, you can keep an eye out for interactions, making sure each member of your team has someone they speak with often and that no one is left sitting alone at lunch. But simplest of all, you can **Q-step**. For example, "How satisfied are you with your relationships at work?" "Who are you closest with at work?" and "Do you feel like you can be your real self at work?"

A great cue to check in on social inclusion is whenever there is a change in people on your team. Use this as an opportunity to have new team experiences and getting-to-know-you conversations, and also discuss social inclusion in your one-on-ones. Help newbies decide who they'd like to spend more time with and what aspect of themselves they want to bring to work more often. Help more tenured team members find ways to get to know and include the newbies. And when a team member leaves, give people one-on-one time to grieve or process their reactions.

If you miss the opportunity to ask about social inclusion at these inflection points (the way Mia did), bring it up anyway, even if several months have passed. Take a look at how Mia broaches the subject in her one-on-one with Kofi:

Version 1: No Do-Over Needed!

Mia: Last time we talked, you brought up that you wish we trusted each other more and did a better job listening. <u>Shall we carve out time to chat about that and our team dynamic in general</u>?

Kofi: I didn't mean to put the team down. I was just frustrated.

Mia: I get that. <u>And I'm hoping we can turn that frustration into an opportunity to work better together and maybe even improve how close you feel to folks on the team</u>.

Kofi: I appreciate that. The truth is . . . you all are so close. I'm used to working with people I know well, and I can't shake feeling like an outsider.

Mia: Thanks for being open about that. It's a tough transition. <u>How about we talk about some ways to feel more like one team</u>?

Aside from team transitions, another good prompt to focus on social inclusion is whenever there is conflict or tension on the team. Use your one-on-ones as an opportunity to **Validate** people's concerns by acknowledging and normalizing how difficult conflict can be, help them clarify their thinking (using **Playbacks**, Split-tracks, and **Deblurring** questions) and come up with ways to address the issue. Help people articulate their needs and invite them to practice giving feedback (see Chapter 9). When you empower your team members to resolve conflict on their own, you will strengthen team cohesion and give people skills and confidence to address problems when they arise.

Lastly, while you can (and should) serve as a catalyst for social inclusion among your team members and others throughout the organization, one of the best predictors of engagement is the connection your team members feel with you as the manager. Employees who say their manager cares about them are significantly more likely to be engaged at work (Harter et al. 2020). So, use your one-on-one time as an opportunity to build a genuine relationship. Ask questions about people's values and interests, do **Playbacks** to show you're really listening, and be willing to share your own. Put in the effort to remember the names of people's family members, significant others, and pets. When people mention something that is important to them, remember it, and follow up about it. To kick-start a Social inclusion check-in in your next one-on-one, pick one of these questions:

Sample Social Inclusion Questions
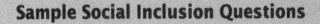

- On a scale of 1–10, how satisfied are you with your sense of social inclusion at work?
- How satisfied are you with how often you collaborate with others?
- How satisfied are you with your sense of belonging on the team?
- Where would you like to be more (or less) included?
- How much of your real self do you get to bring to work?
- Who do you turn to for help? Who else might be a good resource?

(For each question, you can follow up with: What would increase your score by one point?)

Practice Station

That's a wrap for the LifeLabs Learning *CAMPS Model*. Take a moment now to diagnose your own engagement using this tool so you are more likely to remember it. Rate your satisfaction with each of the following at work in the past month:

Certainty   1 2 3 4 5 6 7 8 9 10
Autonomy   1 2 3 4 5 6 7 8 9 10
Meaning   1 2 3 4 5 6 7 8 9 10
Progress   1 2 3 4 5 6 7 8 9 10
Social inclusion 1 2 3 4 5 6 7 8 9 10

Now, let's put it all together. If you haven't already, invite each member of your team to co-create an agenda template that gives them and you ongoing opportunities to track and feed each of the *CAMPS* brain cravings. Tell your team about the *CAMPS* framework to have shared vocabulary. And so that you aren't starting from scratch, check out this sample template:

Sample One-on-One Agenda Template

Goals this quarter	Current results	Projected results

DATE: _____

WINS: What went well or was a highlight this week?
PRIORITIES ALIGNMENT CHECK: My MITs for this week are:
MY CAMPS SCORE (1-10): Fill it in and flag it if there's something you'd like to discuss! Certainty ____ Autonomy ____ Meaning ____ Progress ____ Social inclusion ____
ROADBLOCKS OR CONCERNS: A place I'm stuck or need input is:
DELIBERATE DEVELOPMENT: Individual Development • Skill or knowledge area I am working on: • Action I took last week to build this skill/knowledge area: • Action I will take this week: Feedback • What my manager thinks I did well or could improve: • What I think my manager did well or could improve:
STRETCH QUESTION: Your manager will ask you a different question each time!

ᛘ **Bonus:** For videos of effective one-on-ones, a downloadable agenda template, and our favorite one-on-one stretch questions, visit leaderlab.lifelabslearning.com.

In summary: One-on-ones are a high-leverage tool to diagnose and increase engagement. Schedule frequent, consistent one-on-ones, and co-create an agenda template together. In each conversation, think about your team members' thinking using the LifeLabs Learning *CAMPS Model*: **C**ertainty, **A**utonomy, **M**eaning, **P**rogress, **S**ocial inclusion.

MY LAB REPORT	Today's Date:
My takeaways:	
I regularly hold effective one-on-ones:	1 2 3 4 5 6 7 8 9 10 (strongly disagree) (strongly agree)
Experiment idea bank:	▪ If I'm in a one-on-one meeting, then I'll start by asking about small wins. ▪ If my team member seems disengaged, then I will ask CAMPS questions. ▪ If we're focusing on status updates, then I will suggest a different forum.

One small experiment I'll try to increase my score by 1 point:	
Post-experiment Learning Extractions:	

Bonus: Want to take your manager skills to the next level? Check out the bonus Inclusion Stations at leaderlab.lifelabs-learning.com.

My Learning Tracker

7 out of 7 Core BUs collected. 4 of 8 Core Skills collected.

Q-step	Playback	Deblur	Validate	Linkup	Pause	Extract
Coaching	Feedback	Productivity	1-on-1s			

12

Strategic Thinking

When we train executives across a wide range of industries and countries, we often ask one of our favorite questions: "If you had a magic wand and could equip managers at your company with any skills, which skill would it be?" We hear one answer in reply more than any other. Based on the title of this chapter, we bet you've already guessed what it is: *strategic thinking*.

Similarly, a study of 10,000 senior executives found that they chose strategic thinking as the most important driver of business success 97% of the time, and an assessment of 60,000 managers across over 140 countries revealed that a strategic approach was seen as 1,000% more important to perception of effectiveness than any other behavior (Kabacoff 2014).

Execs are confident that if only the leaders in their companies thought more strategically, their companies would be more successful. But when we ask execs to define strategic thinking, they tend to get stumped. Strategic thinking has the dubious distinction of being one of the most in-demand and one of the most difficult-to-describe leadership skills. It is also an important tipping point skill that unlocks better decision-making, problem-solving, planning, project management, influence, communication, and innovation skills. So, it's time to unveil the mystery. Throughout this chapter, we'll help you and your team develop strategic thinking skills faster to make more impact in less time (and become the stuff that executives dream of).

Let's begin **Deblurring** strategic thinking by learning from contrast. Below is a side-by-side comparison of the average managers versus great managers we studied:

AVERAGE MANAGER BEHAVIORS	GREAT MANAGER BEHAVIORS
Solve today's problems	Also prevent future problems
Wait to be told what to do	Propose new ideas
Act on their first idea	Compare many different ideas
Get their work done	Also improve *how* work gets done

AVERAGE MANAGER BEHAVIORS	GREAT MANAGER BEHAVIORS
Consider the consequences of their actions	Also consider the unintended consequences
React to a problem based on what they see	**Pause** to consider what they might not yet see
Make decisions based on their perspective	Invite and integrate multiple perspectives
Delegate tasks to their team	Articulate what the goals are and why

Drawing on these and similar examples we came across in our research, we noticed two commonalities that characterize the strategic thinking superstars:

1. They **keep the future in mind** when taking action in the present.
2. They **consider the complexities** of any situation.

And great managers don't just hone their own strategic thinking skills. They also help their teams think more strategically. In a word, this kind of thinking is *hard*. It requires an enormous amount of cognitive processing power while your brain attempts to plan for the future by integrating your knowledge of the past and present. And as we've mentioned in past chapters, when people are stressed out and rushing around, this type of thinking is all but impossible. As a result, most teams resort to only occasional bouts of strategic thinking, usually in the form of quarterly or annual planning. But this approach to strategic thinking is far too infrequent in today's world of rapid change, perpetual ambiguity, and interconnected people. Instead, great managers lean on a small set of strategic thinking *habits* they apply themselves and encourage in their team members in everyday decisions and actions. There are dozens of strategic thinking habits and tools out there, but to help you hone this skill and become an even better manager faster, we'll focus on five cornerstone habits that catalyze strategic thinking the fastest.

1. Gap Analysis

Great managers keep the future in mind when taking action in the present and help their teams do it too. So, the first step on any strategic path is figuring out where you actually want to go in the future, then **Deblur** that goal by making it measurable. It is tough, if not impossible, to think strategically with blurry goals like "improve," "reduce," or the ever-popular "optimize." So begin with the end in mind. Next, figure out where you are starting, and make that point measurable as well. We call this essential strategic thinking habit doing a *gap analysis*. Great managers are constantly measuring gaps and instill this gap-tracking habit on their teams.

Start	Gap	Goal

Take a look at the following conversation where Mia misses the opportunity to help Olivia think strategically:

Version 1

Mia: You made a good point recently that our smallest accounts take the most time. I'd love to streamline how we work with them.

Olivia: Me too. I've actually been thinking we should create a bot on our website to answer common questions, so we're spending a lot less time on that.

Mia: Oh, that's interesting. How long do you think it would take us to build it?

Olivia: It would probably take about a month, but I think it would be worth it because we get small questions from clients so often.

Mia:	Okay, that's promising. And how much do you think it would cost us?
Olivia:	I actually think we can get it done for free if we keep it simple.

Even though Mia is asking analytical questions about time and budget, it's still impossible to tell whether the bot idea is the most strategic way to reach their goals. Why? Because neither the goal nor the current situation is clear. There is no *gap analysis*. Skipping this strategic step is akin to hopping on a plane as soon as your friend invites you over to her place. Is the plane the best strategy to get there? It all depends on where your friend lives (the goal), where you live (the current situation), and the gap (the measurable distance between you).

Twenty minutes into a discussion about the website bot, Mia realizes her mistake. She hits her Do-Over Button to try this conversation again, more strategically:

Version 2: Do-Over

Mia:	You made a good point recently that our smallest accounts take the most time. I'd love to streamline how we work with them.
Olivia:	Me too. I've actually been thinking we should create a bot on our website to answer common questions, so we're spending a lot less time on that.

Mia:	Oh, that's interesting. <u>But before we problem-solve, let's do a quick gap analysis.</u> <u>What do you think our goal should be in terms of hours spent on our smallest accounts?</u>
Olivia:	Hm . . . for clients who come to us for a single report, I think we should budget an average of one hour total.
Mia:	Yeah, I agree. <u>So, what's the gap between one hour and how much time we spend now?</u>
Olivia:	Oh, we spend way more time than that now.
Mia:	<u>Let's put some numbers on it so we know how far we are from our goal.</u> <u>How can we make it measurable?</u>
Olivia:	Well, I'm not sure how much time we're actually spending. But a simple way to measure would be to do a time audit this month.

Pausing to do a *gap analysis* quickly results in more thoughtful and effective solutions. This is one of the primary reasons strategic thinking is such a coveted skill on the executive wish-list. Managers who make it a habit to identify and measure gaps (and help their teams do it too) waste less time on the wrong solutions and come up with ideas that are more likely to succeed.

In Mia and Olivia's case, if they discover that the average time spent on small accounts is two hours (with a goal of one hour), they will realize that building a bot is an unnecessarily costly solution. In fact, this gap might be so small that they may decide not to prioritize this area of improvement at all. On the other hand, if they find that the team is spending an average of

10 hours per small account, they might recognize that a bot will not be sufficient. To make a strategic decision about the best path to take, they have to start with a gap analysis. As a bonus, making the gap measurable will also let them monitor progress, course-correct when needed, and celebrate success along the way.

What kinds of metrics are most helpful to measure? Great managers tend to measure gaps on two levels: lead indicators and lag indicators. While lag indicators represent your ulti-mate destination, sometimes these targets are so far in the dis-tance that you need earlier lead indicators to show you if you're on the right track before it's too late to adjust. Here are some examples:

SAMPLE LEAD INDICATOR (EARLY SIGN)	LAG INDICATOR (ULTIMATE GOAL)
Midterm exam grade	Final semester grade
Pop quiz grade	Midterm exam grade
Number of prospects per quarter	Revenue at the end of the year
Post-call client satisfaction score	Number of client referrals
Quarterly engagement survey score	Annual employee retention

The farther away your goal is and the more important it is, the more useful it is to set up multiple *gap analysis* checkpoints along the way. Whether a goal is someone's lag or a lead indica-tor depends on the scope of their role. For example, your head of sales might focus on year-end revenue as her primary objective, while your events manager might focus on the number of attend-ees per month as their primary objective.

Practice Station

Spend a few minutes now strengthening your *gap analysis* muscles. For each of the following goals, come up with several ideas for how you could measure the gap. You don't need a perfect measurement – just something that gives you sufficient guidance to make informed decisions. Then jot down your actual goal and your best guess about the current state:

GOAL	MEASUREMENT IDEAS
Team productivity Goal:	*Sample: average time spent on work versus value of the work* Current state:
Team trust Goal:	*Sample: trust survey, # of times people ask each other for help* Current state:
Your skill as a manager Goal:	*Sample: self-report on scale of 1–10, % of team goals accomplished* Current state:

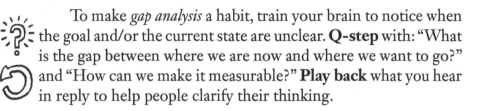

To make *gap analysis* a habit, train your brain to notice when the goal and/or the current state are unclear. **Q-step** with: "What is the gap between where we are now and where we want to go?" and "How can we make it measurable?" **Play back** what you hear in reply to help people clarify their thinking.

2. Linkup

In a dream world, everyone would begin their work with a *gap analysis* and have a crystal clear (and measurable) vision of their destination, but the real world tends to get a lot messier. In our research, we saw that it was surprisingly common for people to find themselves in the midst of a "what" without a clear "why." When great managers recognize they are in this boat, the strategic thinking habit they leverage is to **Link up** and help others do it too.

Take a look at the following conversation between Mia and Kofi. See if you notice the vague links that get in their way of their strategic thinking:

Version 1

Mia: I heard Olivia asked for your help collecting client case studies. Thank you for taking that on. It'll be inspiring for our team. How is it going?

Kofi: Good! I've spent all day working on a template to post the case studies on our website.

Mia: Oh! I didn't realize we were going to post them online. I thought it was more of an internal thing. How many case studies are you trying to develop?

> **Kofi:** I'm aiming for 10 this quarter.
> **Mia:** Wow. That's a lot. How will you have time for your client portfolio or new business?
> **Kofi:** I think I can make it work.
> **Mia:** Okay. Well, thanks for helping out.

 Remember the **Linkup** triangle from Chapter 5? Imagine goals at the top of the triangle and tasks at the bottom. When people rush from one task to the next, it can be easy to lose the link to assume that others are **Linking up** to the same goals as they are.

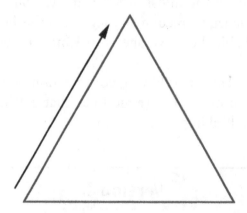

Consider the case of Kofi, Mia, and the case studies. If you drew a triangle representing the case study **Linkup** in Kofi's mind, what goal would you place at the top? In other words, what gap do you think he is hoping to close by creating these case studies? Based on this conversation, your guess is as good as Mia's. If she had a magical thought X-ray machine, or if she just **Q-stepped** with some **Linkup** questions, she would be able to see that she and Kofi are thinking about this project very differently:

KOFI'S IMPLICIT LINKUP		MIA'S IMPLICIT LINKUP	
	3. To improve sales close rate		3. To increase sense of meaning
	2. To build client credibility		2. To show the team's impact
	1. Create case studies		1. Create case studies

Maybe Olivia didn't delegate the assignment well. Maybe Kofi didn't **Q-step** or **Play back** to check for alignment. Whatever the case, he is now driving toward a very different goal than the original intention. **Pausing** to make the implicit **Linkup** explicit would have made this miscommunication clear.

Aside from ensuring alignment, the **Linkup** habit helps you pressure-test people's thinking by asking, "Is this the best way to achieve this goal?" For example, perhaps a more efficient way to give the team a sense of meaning is to invite them to attend client meetings. A better way to improve the sales close rate might be to offer free consultations. **Pausing** to **Linkup** might seem like it slows things down, but it prevents us from going fast in the wrong direction. Besides, even a very short **Linkup Pause** is enough to rapidly kick-start strategic thinking. Take a look at Mia's quick **Linkup** Do-Over with Kofi:

Version 2: Do-Over

Mia: I heard Olivia asked for your help collecting client case studies. Thank you for taking that on. It'll be inspiring for our team. How is it going?

Kofi: Good! I've spent all day working on a template to post the case studies on our website.

Mia: Oh! <u>To make sure we're aligned, would you share what goal you see the case studies linking up to?</u>

Kofi: Well . . . to be honest, I'm not 100% sure. Since we send clients case studies from time to time, I assumed the goal was to close more sales.

Mia: Got it. It makes sense you interpreted it that way. Actually though, Olivia and I thought case studies would be a good way to show our team how much the work we do matters. It was meant to be a small, lightweight project. I'm sorry about the miscommunication.

Kofi: Whoa. I didn't realize that. I get it now.

Mia: <u>So, from your perspective, if the goal is to increase visibility of the impact we have, what's the best way to do this project?</u>

Kofi: Well, the template I made is too complicated for what we need. What about a more lightweight solution like a team chat channel where we share client success stories?

Sometimes, **Linking up** helps people realize they are juggling multiple goals. For example, in Kofi's case, it could be tempting to look for a solution that increases meaning *and* improves the close rate. While it is occasionally possible to kill two birds with one stone (or our much preferred expression: feed two birds with one scone), a single solution that achieves multiple results well is rare. A case study that is polished enough to send to clients might also increase the team's sense of meaning but do so at an unnecessarily high cost. Several professionally produced case studies might improve the close rate, but they won't provide ongoing visibility into the team's impact. The result? Two birds that ate one scone and are both still hungry and cranky. Instead, great managers clarify which goal is the highest priority and create a different **Linkup** map for each one. If you find that rare gem of a solution that achieves multiple goals, go for it. If not, select the best solution to achieve your most important goal.

How much time and effort should you spend considering different paths toward your goal? It all depends on the importance and urgency of the goal and the risks involved in acting too quickly or too slowly. In general, the higher the stakes, the more important it is to **Pause** and **Linkup**.

To make **Linking up** a habit, frequently **Q-step** with: "What does this link up to?" and "Is this the best way to achieve this goal?" When delegating work or assigning responsibilities, **Linkup** to the goal and **Deblur** it.

3. The 3 Lenses Model

As we mentioned at the start of this chapter, strategic thinkers incorporate the *future* into their present decisions, but there is more to it than that. They also consider the *complexities* of any situation. And few situations are more complex than those involving interpersonal problems. Without strong strategic thinking skills, it's easy to miss the many factors involved in interpersonal challenges by simply blaming the people involved. The result? People waste time, effort, and emotions attempting to solve the wrong problems or getting bogged down in destructive conflict. By some estimates, unproductive conflict costs companies an average of $359 billion per year (Hayes 2008). By contrast, great managers resolve interpersonal problems faster by looking at them through multiple lenses. We call this strategic thinking habit the *3 Lenses Model.* To adopt this habit, look at any person-related problem through three lenses, and help your team members do it too:

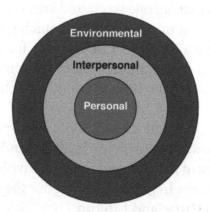

Source: LifeLabs Learning.

- **Lens #1: Personal.** Ask: "How are they contributing to the situation?" For example, does this person lack the skill or will necessary to achieve this goal?
- **Lens #2: Interpersonal.** Ask: "How am I contributing to the situation?" For example, have I failed to set clear expectations or model and reinforce the desired behavior?
- **Lens #3: Organizational.** Ask: "How is our team and/or company contributing to the situation?" For example, are there resource constraints or problematic org-wide norms?

Without a quick *3 Lenses* analysis, you can easily miss the complexities of a situation and overlook creative solutions. As a case in point, take a look at another exchange between Mia with Olivia later in the week:

Version 1

Mia: How have things been going with Jeff in Finance?

Olivia: Well, he's been more willing to help since I set up time for us to understand each other's work a little better. So that's a relief. But when I come to him with a problem, his first reaction is still to get defensive and blame it on our team. It's frustrating. I realize some of their work didn't end up getting used, so maybe he's still annoyed about that. But, honestly, he was difficult to work with even before that happened. He's just one of those rigid people.

Mia: That sounds tough. What do you think you can do about it?

Why do you think Olivia is butting heads with Jeff despite her best efforts to improve their relationship? Based on this conversation, it's hard to say, and Mia's question is premature. She's missing out on an opportunity to help Olivia **Pause** and think strategically about the different factors that may be contributing to Jeff's behavior. Keeping the *3 Lenses Model* in mind, Mia goes back in time with the help of her Do-Over Button to help Olivia diagnose the situation more strategically:

Version 2: Do-Over

Mia: How have things been going with Jeff in Finance?

Olivia: Well, he's been more willing to help since I set up time for us to understand each other's work a little better. So that's a relief. But when I come to him with a problem, his first reaction is still to get defensive and blame it on our team. It's frustrating. I realize some of their work didn't end up getting used, so maybe he's still annoyed about that. But, honestly, he was difficult to work with even before that happened. He's just one of those rigid people.

Mia: That sounds tough. <u>Would it help if we analyzed it through a few different lenses?</u>

Olivia: What do you mean?

Mia: Well, we can look at the problem through the lens of Jeff's personality or communication style, but that's hard to change. <u>So I'm curious if we get any new insights by looking through other lenses. For example, are there ways you or I might be contributing to his behavior?</u>

Olivia: Oh, interesting. Well, I guess one way I'm contributing is that I come to him with problems pretty last minute, and by then I'm already stressed out. I imagine that's frustrating.

Mia: Yeah, that's a good insight. Anything else?

Olivia: Until this past month, I didn't spend any time getting to know him or his team. That's something I can keep getting better at.

Mia:	<u>And what if we look at it through an organizational lens? Is there anything about how our teams work together or the company as a whole that might be impacting him?</u>
Olivia:	Well, there's the possibility of the merger, so I'm guessing that's made things really busy in the Finance department. They're probably short-staffed.
Mia:	Yeah, good point.
Olivia:	Plus there's no process in place to ask Finance for help, so different people must be coming to them with all sorts of different requests in different ways.
Mia:	Based on what you've considered, what comes to mind as new solutions to test out?
Olivia:	Well, I'm realizing I should involve Finance earlier, so we're not all rushing. And in my next conversation with Jeff, I can ask if there is a process he prefers we use with them.

Practice Station

Take a moment now and think of an interpersonal conflict or tension you have with someone. Write out what might be impacting this person's behavior using the *3 Lenses Model*:

Lens #1: Personal. Are they missing necessary skills or the will to change?

Lens #2: Interpersonal. Are you contributing to the problem?

Lens #3: Organizational. Are there other contributing factors in the environment?

Next, come up with one new solution to test out that you haven't tried yet.

 To get in the habit of using the *3 Lenses Model*, as soon as you detect interpersonal tension, **Pause** and **Q-step** with: "What are the different factors that might be contributing to this situation?" Be sure to **Play back** what you hear to help folks clarify their thoughts.

4. UC Check

While average managers do tend to think through the consequences of their actions and help their team do so too, great managers go even further to ensure everyone is thinking strategically. They develop a habit we like to call doing an *UC Check* (pronounced Uck!): they check for *unintended* consequences.

Before we explain how *UC Checks* work, let's first consider the story of the Hawaiian mongoose. In 1883, Hawaiian sugar cane plantation owners had a problem. Rats were destroying their crops. In an attempt to find an organic solution, they imported 72 mongooses to control the rat population, then shipped baby mongooses across a variety of Hawaiian islands. The mongooses did eat the rats, but they also ate birds and insects that pollinated the crops. By now, the mongooses and their offspring have cost Hawaiian farmers tens of millions of dollars in damages (Gamayo 2016). How did the little mongoose become such a big problem? Everyone involved focused on the desirable consequences (fewer rats) and nobody did an *UC Check* to anticipate the unintended (and undesirable) consequences.

Why is it so easy to forget those pesky *UCs*? Human brains easily fall victim to the confirmation bias – a tendency to search for evidence supporting one's perspective while ignoring contradictory evidence. When people are excited about a solution, it's difficult for them to see any information that disconfirms their beliefs. Great managers know this and nudge themselves and others to anticipate what might go wrong.

Practice Station

Put on your most pessimistic, future-proofing glasses and consider the unintended consequences of the following actions. What might go wrong? Who might be impacted?

ACTION	UNINTENDED CONSEQUENCES
You designate Fridays as a meeting-free day.	*Sample: Coworkers in some time zones have too little time together.*

ACTION	UNINTENDED CONSEQUENCES
You film and share all company meetings.	*Sample: People miss important announcements because the videos are too long to watch.*
You only hire college graduates.	*Sample: You narrow your candidate pool and limit your team's diversity.*
You host a team retreat in Hawaii.	*Sample: Coworkers with young children can't attend. Mongooses eat all your birds.*

The goal of the *UC Check* is not to avoid taking action but to shine a light on unseen consequences so you can take even more thoughtful and strategic action. Once you identify risks and possible negative impacts, you can consider how you might mitigate these consequences. In some cases, the result might be choosing a different solution (please, no more mongooses!). In other cases, the *UC Check* will guide you to do more research or tweak your plan – for example, involving more people or running a pilot before a full launch.

As we mentioned in Chapter 7, another great tool to anticipate unintended consequences is the pre-mortem. Unlike a *post*-mortem, which helps people **Extract** lessons after a problem occurs, a *pre*-mortem starts with the premise that something will go wrong, before it actually does. To run a pre-mortem, invite impacted stakeholders to imagine that a project or decision was a failure, then ask: "What caused things to go wrong?" and "What can we do today to prevent these problems in the future?" Research shows that the practice of "prospective hindsight" increases ability to identify unintended consequences by 30% (Mitchell, Russo, and Pennington 1989).

To get in the habit of doing *UC Checks*, ask yourself and others the following questions before making a decision or introducing a change:

- "What might be the unintended consequences?"
- "What might the risks be?"
- "Who might be negatively impacted?"
- "How might we mitigate the UC?"

5. Inclusive Planning

Of all the strategic errors we've discussed so far, research shows that one is worse than all the rest: not including the right people at the right times (Neilson, Martin, and Powers 2008). While on the surface this seems like an easy mistake to fix, the solution tends to get complicated. How can you ensure that you aren't forgetting to include someone? What if you include too many people? At what point in a project or decision should each person get involved? The good news is that one strategic habit simplifies this complexity and helps you and your team make good decisions faster. We call it *inclusive planning*.

The first part of practicing *inclusive planning* is to break up a project or decision into distinct phases. In most cases, the project phases will include the following:

Inclusive Planning Grid				
Phase 1 Define goal	Phase 2 Analyze problem	Phase 3 Explore solutions	Phase 4 Pick solution	Phase 5 Execute

Phase 1 is all about doing a *gap analysis* by **Deblurring** your end point and start point and making them measurable.

Phase 2 is an opportunity to diagnose the current problem or situation using the *3 Lenses Model*.

Phase 3 is the point at which you'll want to generate many ideas to close the gap (we'll share idea generating pro-tips in the next chapter).

Phase 4 is when you narrow your options and select one solution (stay tuned for tips on how to do this well in the next chapter). This is also a good time to do an *UC Check*.

Phase 5 is the point at which you actually execute on the plan.

All along the way, **Linkup** to ensure the goal stays clear to everyone involved.

Notice that each phase of the process creates an opportunity to **Pause** and invite your strategic thinking habits to the party. When you break down work into these phases, it also allows you to **Deblur** who should be involved at each point. Looking back on the many times Luca has felt excluded since Mia has been manager, *inclusive planning* could have been the ideal solution.

Practice Station

Take a look at the *Inclusive Planning* grid and predict what will go wrong:

Stake-holders	Phase 1 Define goal	Phase 2 Analyze problem	Phase 3 Explore solutions	Phase 4 Pick solution	Phase 5 Execute
Ally	X	X	X	X	
Jorge	X	X		X	
Rio					X

> Even at a glance, you likely noticed that Rio (the person doing all the executing) is getting involved much too late in the process. There are bound to be challenges Ally and Jorge did not anticipate, and Rio will feel little ownership over the work. Ally also misses out on benefiting from diverse perspectives in the exploration phase. And having two people involved in Phase 4, making the ultimate decision, might cause confusion and delays without a plan for what they will do if they disagree.

To determine who you should involve at each phase and develop an *inclusive planning* habit, ask yourself and others these questions:

- "Who will be impacted by this?"
- "Who will have to execute on the plan?"
- "Who might be a vocal advocate or detractor?"
- "Who might have relevant insider scoop or expertise?"
- "Whose perspective might we be overlooking?"

Once you decide who should be involved at each phase, make your plan visible. In this way, you'll help your stakeholders understand how, when, and why they will be asked to contribute. If someone believes they should be included in a different phase, you'll have the opportunity to **Pause, Extract** the learning, explain your reasoning, and course-correct, if needed.

***

In summary: Strategic thinking entails considering the future and the complexities of any situation. A handful of strategic thinking habits helps managers and teams make better decisions: *Gap analysis*, **Linkup**, *3 Lenses Model*, *UC Check*, and *Inclusive Planning*.

MY LAB REPORT	Today's Date:
My takeaways:	
I regularly think strategically:	1 2 3 4 5 6 7 8 9 10 (strongly disagree) (strongly agree)
Experiment idea bank:	■ If someone suggests an improvement idea, then I will ask about their gap analysis. ■ If I notice interpersonal tension, then I will diagnose it using the 3 Lenses Model. ■ If I am starting a project, then I will create and share an inclusive planning grid.
One small experiment I'll try to increase my score by 1 point:	
Post-experiment Learning Extractions:	

Bonus: Want to take your manager skills to the next level? Check out the bonus Inclusion Stations at leaderlab.lifelabs-learning.com.

My Learning Tracker

7 out of 7 Core BUs collected. 5 of 8 Core Skills collected.

Q-step	Play-back	Deblur	Validate	Linkup	Pause	Extract
Coaching	Feed-back	Produc-tivity	1-on-1s	Strategic Thinking		

13

Meetings Mastery

A bittersweet fact about life is that it is short. Time is precious. So it's startling to realize that the average employee spends 20–40% of their work time in meetings. Throughout a typical career, that's up to *four years of life* spent in a meeting. This isn't a bad thing in and of itself. Meetings can be where we come together to achieve great things. We can engineer new ideas together. We can learn from each other. We can celebrate together. We can help one another make tough decisions. We can feel the camaraderie of laboring side by side to achieve goals we couldn't reach alone. Great managers know how to lead great meetings like these.

Alas, most people say that about *half* of their meetings are a waste of time (Rogelberg 2019). In case you weren't keeping count, that's about two consecutive wasted years of life. Bad meetings also drain energy, creativity, engagement, and money. A study of 19 million meetings found that bad meetings cost the participating companies *half a trillion dollars* – that's 11 zeroes worth of money (Doodle 2019). This is sad news. But the good news is that we've seen managers learn to rapidly achieve *meetings mastery* and pass on these skills to their team. Leading meetings well is also a tipping point skill that spills over into better communication, influence, decision-making, inclusion, productivity, negotiation, conflict resolution, and public speaking.

Let's begin with a look at a typical meeting on Mia's team. Then, throughout this chapter, we'll take this meeting from average to great. We'll also equip you with a small but mighty set of tools great managers use to lead great meetings, including how to start strong, select the right meeting tools, and course-correct when things go wrong. You can apply these tools right away and pass them on to others so we can all spend our lives in better meetings.

Version 1

Mia: Hey, everyone. As you know, we're creating client categories so we can prioritize how we spend our time. I was hoping to hear your thoughts on what the categories should be.

Olivia: I think we keep it simple, like small, medium, and large.

Luca: That doesn't really work though. What if it's a small client with big potential?

Kofi: Well, at my last company –

Olivia: I wasn't implying that it's just about their current size. I just mean we should come up with three categories.

Luca: Maybe before we decide on what to call the categories we should talk about how we would change our levels of service? Otherwise the categories are meaningless.

Olivia: Well, the problem is that we're treating all clients equally right now, and some of them take a lot more of our time than others.

Starting Meetings: 4P Opener

One of the fastest ways to make every meeting that you have from now on better is to start strong. The first few minutes of any meeting predict the quality of the meeting as a whole. So what does it take to start well? Based on our observations of what great managers do differently (adapted from Whetten & Cameron, 1991), we refer to the formula for great meeting kickoffs as the *4P Opener*. When starting a meeting, great managers share these four components:

1. **Purpose:** Why the meeting is happening.
   Example: "The purpose of this meeting is to [update, explore, decide, etc.]"

   This first P **Links up** to the goal of the meeting, ensuring it is a strategic use of time. Without a Purpose statement, conversations will pull in different directions, causing confusion, frustration, and inefficiency. Clarifying Purpose up front also helps participants focus on the topic at hand instead of getting distracted by thoughts from their previous meetings.

2. **Product:** What the group will have at the end of the meeting that didn't exist at the start.
   Example: "We will leave here with [five ideas, a decision, a list of next steps, etc.]"
   While Purpose provides a broad focus area, the next P – Product – creates a mental progress bar in everyone's minds toward the ultimate result of this specific meeting. The more tangible the Product, the more likely people will be to hold each other and themselves accountable for staying on topic. As we discussed in Chapter 11, progress is a major driver of engagement (it is the P in *CAMPS*). If you want your meeting participants to be engaged, make sure the Product is clear and that you make steady progress toward it throughout the meeting.

3. **Personal benefit:** The reason meeting participants will feel motivated to contribute.
   Example: "This will help you/us [save time, feel aligned, make an impact, etc.]"
   A Personal benefit statement ignites people's sense of meaning – another necessary ingredient for engagement that we introduced in Chapter 11 (the M in *CAMPS*). The Personal benefit statement should spark motivation to achieve the Product. Without an explicit Personal benefit, it can be easy for people to "check out" and become passive bystanders.

A Personal benefit statement also gives you, as the meeting leader, an opportunity to **Linkup** to why you are passionate about this topic. Research shows that the meeting leader's mood at the start of a meeting acts as a positive or negative contagion for the rest of the participants (Rogelberg 2019). When you are excited about the meeting topic, your team is more likely to get excited too.

4. **Process:** How will we structure the conversation?
   Example: "We'll spend the first half on agenda point X, and the second half on point Y."
   The final P – Process – outlines how the group will achieve the Product. Ideally, this takes the form of an agenda shared in advance of the meeting and again at the beginning. Research shows that agendas rapidly improve meeting quality (Cohen et al. 2011). Several of our clients have even adopted a "no agenda, no attenda" rule company-wide. To maintain focus, keep your agenda visible throughout the meeting. To spark more dopamine, check off each item on the agenda as you complete it. And to build time awareness skills (see Chapter 10), write time estimates for each agenda item, then record how long each item actually took. Aside from the agenda, you can also clarify other Process points like ground rules and instructions for how to use any relevant meeting technology.

Sample Meeting Agenda

Meeting 4Ps:

   Purpose: Help our Facilities Team select a new office location

   Product: A list of our top five office recommendations

   Personal benefit: Move into an office we're excited to come to every day!

> **Process:** See agenda below. <u>Meeting norms</u>: *share the floor; help get all voices into the conversation; stay present; no multitasking; off-topic points go in the parking lot*
>
> 1. Share one thing you like about our current office *[30 seconds each, 3 minutes total]*
> 2. Review the list of office options in silence and jot down your questions *[5 minutes]*
> 3. Discuss office questions *[15 minutes]*
> 4. Vote on our top office picks to get the list down to five *[2 minutes]*

The *4P Opener* is an indispensable meeting tool because it creates focus, progress, and motivation at the very start and allows you to course-correct if the meeting ever goes off track.

You can even use the *4Ps* to set up your meeting for success *before* you schedule it. Don't gather people until you have **Paused** to **Deblur** your Purpose and Product. In some cases, articulating the *4Ps* out loud will help you realize that you don't need a meeting at all (perhaps an email will meet your goals more efficiently). Use the Personal benefit check to ensure you are inviting the right people (see the *inclusive planning* framework in Chapter 12 to make this decision strategically). And share the Process beforehand so everyone shows up ready to contribute. Sharing your *4Ps* in advance of the meeting also gives people a chance to decide whether they should attend. Another terrific meeting norm several of our clients have adopted is "It's fine to decline!" If you want better quality

meetings, be sure to **Validate** thoughtful opt outs by normalizing that it's common (or not a problem) to decline. When the *4Ps* are clear before and during the meeting, people can be more strategic about their time and become better meeting participants faster. Let's take a look at how Mia opens her meeting with the *4Ps*, thanks to her Do-Over Button:

Version 2: Do-Over

Mia: Hey, everyone. As you know, we've decided to create client categories so we can better prioritize how we spend our time. So, the <u>purpose of this meeting is</u> to gather your ideas on criteria we should use to create these categories. <u>By the end of the meeting</u>, I'd like to have a list of at least 20 possible factors to consider. Then we can meet on Monday to narrow the list. Having these categories <u>will make all of our lives easier</u> since we'll have clear client service priorities and guidelines. <u>The process I'd like to follow today</u> is to silently jot down our ideas, share out loud, then open the floor to build on each other's ideas. Kofi will be the notetaker and Luca will be the timekeeper to keep us on track. How does that sound?

Use the *4P Opener* whenever you are leading a meeting, and support others by **Q-stepping** with *4P* questions and using **Playbacks** to ensure alignment. For example, "Just so I know how best to contribute, would you share what we're hoping to accomplish in this meeting?" and "Thanks for inviting me. So that I can prepare, would you let me know the agenda?"

Practice Station

Pick a meeting you will be leading in the near future. Write down your *4P Opener:*

Purpose:

Product:

Personal benefit:

Process:

Now that your meeting has gotten off to a strong start, the next thing to ensure is that it stays productive. To do this well, great managers stock their meeting toolboxes with a variety of tools. We'll share our favorite tools with you now, but first it's important to return to P #1 of the *4P Opener*. Selecting the right meeting tools starts with understanding the Purpose of your meeting or meeting segment. The most common meeting purposes are:

- **Inform:** share information, news, thoughts, and/or feelings; answer questions
- **Explore:** ask questions; generate ideas; spark insights
- **Narrow:** debate; prioritize; vote; decide; determine a plan of action

When we ask our workshop participants which meeting type they most enjoy, the rooms tend to be starkly divided between the "explorers" and the "narrowers." Some people delight in generating new ideas, and others relish the closure of making a decision. This diversity of preferences can be a major strength, but only when it is harnessed well. Without skillful meeting facilitation, the explorers pull to keep considering new ideas while the narrows diligently shoot them down. Here's a snippet of the prototypical explorer–narrower dynamic:

> **Explorer:** *Oh! Another option we haven't considered yet is changing our work hours.*
>
> **Narrower:** *That would never work. People won't agree to a different schedule.*
>
> **Explorer:** *It might be interesting to research industries where that's the norm.*
>
> **Narrower:** *But in our industry that wouldn't be realistic.*

Without a **Deblurred** meeting purpose, it's easy for everyone to pull in the direction of their preferred meeting type. The result is what we call "entanglement" – when your meeting starts to look like a random bundle of cords hiding away in some forgotten drawer. Once you are clear on the meeting purpose, it's time to select some good tools for that type of meeting. Below, we share some of the most helpful tools we've come across in our research on great managers.

"Inform" Meeting Tools

Let's be real, an Inform-type meeting is most at risk of being a bore. In fact, one study found that nearly 50% of participants would rather do a variety of unpleasant activities (including watch paint dry) than attend a "status update" meeting (Howard 2015). If your meeting is going to be a one-way data-dump without interaction, you can save everyone time by sending an asynchronous message instead (for example, presentation, video, email). That said, there are several good uses for this type of meeting if you leverage these three tools:

"Inform" Meeting Tool #1: Q-Storm

One of the more fruitful uses of Inform meetings is *Q&A* (Question and Answer) meetings or meeting segments. These are gatherings that give your meeting participants a chance to **Q-step** on a specific topic or, in the case of "AMAs" (Ask Me Anything sessions), questions about any topic at all. To help everyone get the best use of this time, provide information in advance so people have a chance to process it on their own. Then invite participants to do a *q-storm*, which is the question version of a brainstorm, where everyone generates interesting **Q-step** ideas together. Here's how it all comes together:

1. Designate a document or a tool where everyone can submit their questions.
2. Before the Q&A or AMA, ask everyone to vote on the most important questions.
3. Prepare your answers in advance so you can present information that is **Deblurred** and **Links up** to goals and personal benefits – but leave room for participants to ask clarifying questions in real time.

4. Answer questions that received the most votes, and let people know how to follow up with you if their question wasn't chosen.

You can do *q-storming* sessions where you give answers, invite different team members to lead Q&As about work they are doing, and invite internal and external stakeholders as special guests.

"Inform" Meeting Tool #2: Round-robins

Another valuable Inform meeting variety is the daily or weekly team huddle. The purpose of a huddle is multifaceted, including aligning on priorities, creating shared accountability, quickly flagging and removing roadblocks, and building team trust and cohesion thanks to the mere-exposure effect (first introduced in Chapter 11). A meeting facilitation tool that helps you get the most out of your huddles is the *round-robin*.

A *round-robin* (which comes from the French word for "ribbon") is a process of going around to **Pause** and hear from each person in the group. Not only are *round-robins* efficient because you don't have to wait around and wonder who will speak next, they also help you harness the collective wisdom of your team, instead of letting just a few voices run the show. Research shows that equal conversational turn-taking is a better predictor of team performance than even collective team member IQ (Woolley et al. 2010). So when you do *round-robins*, be sure to give everyone equal speaking time – unless someone on your team tells you they have a speech difference that requires more time. Pro-tip: use an audible timer so people can self-monitor their talking time or a video call plug-in that shows participants how long each person has been speaking.

A *round-robin* is a helpful tool whenever you want to hear from everyone in the group, and it is especially useful at the start of meetings. When you get people's voices in the room early on, they will be more likely to contribute throughout the meeting. Even research on surgical teams shows that doing a *round-robin* before surgery makes it more likely that team members speak up and point out potential errors in the midst of the procedure, leading complications and deaths to decline by 35% (Gawande 2009). *Round-robins* save lives, and they can save your next meeting. Here are some of the most common *round-robin* prompts we've seen great managers use in their team huddles:

- "What is one win, frustration, or learning **Extraction** from the past week/yesterday?"
- "What did you accomplish yesterday?"
- "What are you working on today/what is your MIT?"
- "What are your roadblocks or obstacles?"

If someone brings up an obstacle, beware of meeting entanglement. If the purpose of the meeting is just to inform, be sure to take the problem-solving conversation off-line. And since huddles have little interaction other than listening to one another, keep these meetings short and high-energy. The great managers we studied did this in many creative ways from starting and ending with music or a group cheer to holding standing or walking meetings if all team members were able to participate. It turns out standing meetings are generally 34% shorter without sacrificing meeting quality (Bluedorn, Turban, and Love 1999).

"Inform" Meeting Tool #3: Rotate Roles

Even though a quick image search for the words "leader" or "manager" brings up countless depictions of leaders at the front of the room telling people what to do, the great managers we studied were very different. If we were to show you photos of their team meetings, you wouldn't be able to pick out the manager in the photo. To quote the philosopher Lao Tzu, "Leaders are best when people barely know they exist. When their work is done, their aim fulfilled, people will say, 'We did it ourselves.'" How do great managers bring this ancient wisdom to life in the modern world? One very simple way to do this within meetings is to regularly *rotate roles*.

While average managers generally lead all their team meetings, the great managers we studied were far more likely to ask team members to take turns leading. Common roles to rotate include:

- Facilitating
- Timekeeping
- Note taking and sending minutes
- Room setup and breakdown

Rotating roles gives everyone an opportunity to be visible, enables sharing of administrative responsibilities, and teaches folks to be better meeting participants by building empathy for all roles. As a bonus, each person brings their own "flavor" to these roles, creating variety in what could otherwise become a monotonous meeting. For even more rapid meeting improvement, encourage team members to **Pause** and **Extract** learnings from their experiences by pulling for feedback.

"Explore" Meeting Tools

While Inform meetings are all about a simple exchange of information, the purpose of Explore meetings is to generate new insights and ideas together. Over the years, these types of meetings have grown in popularity, but sadly, research shows that they are usually less productive than coming up with ideas solo (Rickards 1999). So how can you avoid the common pitfalls of these meetings and harness their power? First, ensure that you are setting aside time for silent, solo ideation as well as group ideation (including dyad and large-group exploration). Then, throughout the meeting, lean on the following meeting tools:

"Explore" Meeting Tool #1: Defer Judgment

Imagine you are leading an experiment, and assign two groups of people a problem to solve. You instruct one group to come up with good ideas. You instruct the other group to *defer judgment* – suspend any evaluation of their ideas until after the exercise except for some **Validating** comments along the way. What do you expect to find when you look over their answers? This is exactly what researchers Sidney Parnes and Arnold Meadow (1959) wanted to find out in their now-classic study on creativity. It turns out the people who were told to come up with good ideas did worse than the judgment-free group. In fact, the group that deferred judgment generated twice as many good ideas. Why? The part of the brain responsible for evaluating ideas actually blocks the part of the brain responsible for generating ideas. In short, we can't do both at once well.

The great managers we studied actively reminded people to *defer judgment*, even if they were generating ideas in silence. And when exploring ideas out loud, they pointed out any critiques or even excessive praise that could switch on the group's judgment filters. Here is a snippet of a sample conversation:

> ***Explorer:*** *Oh! Another option we haven't considered yet is changing our work hours.*
>
> ***Narrower:*** *That would never work. People won't agree to a different schedule.*

Meeting facilitator: Whoops. That sounds like an evaluation of the idea. Can you hang onto that concern until we start narrowing down our options?

The goal of an exploration session shouldn't be to generate good ideas only. Actually, some of the wildest ideas can spark some of the best solutions. For example, consider the story of a major innovation at the Pacific Power and Light company, PP&L (Camper 1993). PP&L had a big employee safety, recruitment, and retention problem in the role responsible for clearing power transmission lines after storms. It was a dangerous job, and few people were willing to do it, but it had to be done. So PP&L put together a think tank of employees with diverse backgrounds to generate ideas. Joking around, one person suggested training bears to climb up poles and shake the lines clean of ice. Building on the idea, someone else said they could place honey pots on top of the poles to attract the bears. But how would they get the honey pots onto the poles? Someone suggested having helicopters fly over the poles to drop them off. All still very silly stuff – until a secretary who had previously worked in a field hospital pointed out that helicopter blades could actually blow the ice and snow right off the power lines. Ever since that meeting, PP&L has been using helicopters to do just that.

"Explore" Meeting Tool #2: Idea Quotas

Want an easy shortcut to helping people be less judgy? Assign an *idea quota*. For example, set a goal of generating 10 ideas in 10 minutes or have teams compete over who will come up with more ideas. Paradoxically, a focus on quantity leads to higher quality. An *idea quota* also helps push people beyond boring, surface-level solutions. It keeps people digging even after they think their idea wells have dried up.

Practice Station

Practice deferring judgment and working toward an *idea quota*. Right now, set a timer for four minutes, and come up with at least twelve ways to improve your company meetings.

"Explore" Meeting Tool #3: Cross-pollinate

In their book *Innovation as Usual*, authors Paddy Miller and Thomas Wedell-Wedellsborg (2013) share the story of a large organization that wanted to find out which of their employees were most innovative. To their surprise, they found that most of the innovators shared one trait: they were *smokers*. Was it that nicotine was somehow fueling creativity? Fortunately, no. The organization was very compartmentalized, and most employees never really connected to people from other departments. But the smokers did just that in the shared smoking break area. Their smoking habit helped them connect regularly with colleagues from all over the business. It was these spontaneous collisions of thoughts and skills that sparked original ideas.

The best managers we studied recognized the power of bringing people with diverse backgrounds and views together. They made their exploration meetings better faster by deliberately *cross-pollinating* people's perspectives. Just as cross-pollination gives life to brand new varieties of plants, it also gives life to brand new ideas. Sometimes diversity is helpful because someone in the room happens to have a unique lens that is relevant for the problem at hand (like the secretary at PP&L who was familiar with helicopters). But even without specific subject matter expertise, more diversity leads to better outcomes simply because different views coming together result in new ways of thinking. What's more, research shows that groups that have visible diversity (in characteristics such as race, age, and gender) are more curious about one another's perspectives because they assume that people with different identities will think differently, regardless of whether or not they actually do (Phillips, Northcraft, and Neale 2006).

 To become a great cross-pollinator faster, get in the habit of **Q-stepping** with questions like:

- "Whose perspective might we be missing?"
- "Do we have enough diversity of people and perspectives in the room?"
- "What other people, departments, companies, industries, or even species have solved a similar problem? What can we learn from them?"

"Narrow" Meeting Tools

Once you generate a variety of options in divergent thinking mode, you'll have to narrow your options in convergent thinking mode. As we shared in Chapter 10, the word "decide" comes from the Latin for "to cut off." So while success for an Explore-type meeting is about creating *more*, success in a Narrow-type meeting is all about moving toward *less*.

When possible, we suggest doing exploring and narrowing work in two separate meetings. First, in most cases it will make sense to have fewer people in the room for the narrowing conversation. Second, research shows that different states of mind are conducive to different types of thinking (Pope 2016; Wieth and Zacks 2011). For most people, novel thinking is easier later in the day when they are tired and less likely to self-censor, and decision-making is most effective in the morning when the brain's serotonin and dopamine levels are higher (Shiv et al. 2005). Much like the writing advice that often goes "Write drunk, edit sober," when it comes to meetings, you'll want to help your team explore playfully and decide seriously. How do you quickly improve the quality of your narrowing meetings? The following are three helpful tools.

 ### "Narrow" Meeting Tool #1: Deblur the DACI

Many of the great managers we studied used some kind of decision-making framework with their teams in general and especially during narrowing meetings. One of our favorites is the *DACI Model*, which stands for:

- **Driver:** the person "behind the wheel" of an initiative who is responsible for getting it across the finish line. Just as in a car, there should only be one driver.
- **Approver(s):** the person or people who make the final decision. Sometimes the Driver and Approver are the same person.
  - *Important: If there are multiple approvers, make the Approval Process explicit: for example, single approver, two approvers and a tiebreaker if needed, consensus (all agree to support the decision), majority vote (51%).*
- **Consultants:** people who provide input, suggestions, feedback, or execute components of the work.
- **Informed:** people who are updated along the way and when the work is done.

The beauty of *DACI* (and similar models) is that it helps you and your team make implicit expectations explicit. Without a clear Approver and Approval Process, debates can range indefinitely and the loudest voices typically win out. To make an immediate improvement in the quality of your Narrow meetings, **Pause** to **Deblur** the *DACI* and Approval Process from the start or **Q-step** and **Play back** to help others articulate the *DACI*.

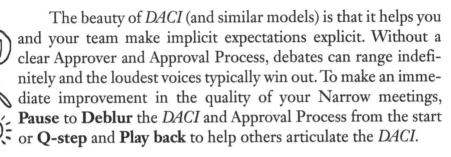

Practice Station

Pop quiz! Pick a project or initiative someone on your team is leading, and do a *DACI* check. Are the **D**river, **A**pprover(s), **C**onsultant(s), and **I**nformed roles all clear? Does the person leading the project agree? Does the Driver know when to loop in others?

"Narrow" Meeting Tool #2: Impact/Feasibility Map

Once everyone is clear on how the decision will be made, it's time to do the work of moving toward the decision. If you've already generated a wide range of ideas, a helpful tool to narrow the list is an *Impact/Feasibility Map*. Here's how it works:

- Write each idea the team generated on a separate physical or digital "sticky note."
- Combine all the ideas.
- Remove any duplicates.

- Plot each idea on the spectrum of *Impact* (how likely it will be that the idea achieves the desired result) and *Feasibility* (how realistic it will be to act on this idea given existing constraints – like time, money, and the team's skill level).

For example, in this chart, imagine your team's goal is to double the number of attendees for the next conference. Idea **A** might be to invite an A-list celebrity. It would probably have a big impact, but it is not feasible given your budget. Idea **B** might be to rename the conference. It would be easy, but it is unlikely to have a significant impact. Idea **C** is the sweet spot (high impact and high feasibility) – for example, letting attendees purchase a second ticket for 50% off.

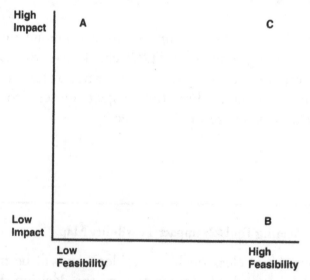

Source: LifeLabs Learning.

The goal of this exercise is not to have complete agreement or even to know for sure how to categorize each idea. The point is to narrow your list of ideas down to those that are most likely to succeed and to hear people's reasoning in the process. While Impact and Feasibility are the most common criteria, you can also do this exercise with other criteria (like speed versus cost, aesthetics versus functionality, convenience versus environmental impact).

"Narrow" Meeting Tool #3: Pros, Cons, and Mitigations

After your large list dwindles down to a small list of feasible, high-impact ideas, it's easy for debate to ensue. Constructive conflict can be a terrific force for ensuring that decisions are thoughtful and strategic, but conflict can also easily turn personal. One of our favorite tools to keep conflict helpful is articulating the *pros, cons, and mitigations* for each idea. The brilliance of this framework is that, instead of having people debate one another, you turn the team's focus toward the ideas. Here's how it works, one idea at a time:

1. **Pros:** Going *round-robin*, each person shares what they see as the idea's pros, strengths, and advantages.
2. **Cons:** Each person shares what they see as the cons, risks, and disadvantages of the idea. (This is a great time to use the *UC Check* habit we introduced in the last chapter to consider unintended consequences on the business and on individuals not in the room.)
3. **Mitigations** Each person proposes mitigation suggestions to amplify the pros and reduce the impact of the cons.

In this way, your team adopts an "us versus the problem" rather than a "me versus you" mindset. One of the great managers we interviewed for our research at LifeLabs Learning took this philosophy so seriously that he even insisted that his team members all sat together on the same side of the table, with a whiteboard on the opposite side – illustrating their commitment to debating the issues rather than the individuals.

Course Corrections

Before we bring this chapter to a close, we want to acknowledge that sometimes no matter how well you start your meetings or select your meeting tools, your meeting can still go off track. Some people will ramble endlessly. Some people will stay silent.

Some will frolic off topic, taking the rest of the team with them. How do you handle this endless array of meeting challenges and surprises? And if you are rotating facilitator responsibilities on your team (and we hope you are), how do you help your team members know what to do?

Based on our analysis of hundreds of meeting hours (including department meetings, team meetings, all hands, executive teams, and cross-functional groups), we noticed that the best managers and meeting leaders are skilled at *course-correcting*. To get good at this subtle meeting art faster, use the following course-correction formula:

Behavior observation + impact statement + process suggestion

The first two parts of the formula are essentially the B and I of the *Q-BIQ Method* we shared in Chapter 10. It is a judgment-free and **Deblurred** description of the behavior happening within the meeting and a **Linkup** to the impact it's having. Once you **Pause** to articulate what you see, make a process suggestion to bring the meeting back on track (for example, by recommending one of the tools we've shared in this chapter).

Practice Station

Here are some common meeting challenges. For each one, practice what you would say to course-correct, including a behavior observation, impact statement, and process suggestion. Compare your answer to the sample course corrections we provide:

Meeting Challenge	Sample Course Correction
There is very little discussion.	*It seems we're quiet today, which means it's hard to tell if we're aligned. How about we take five minutes to q-storm in silence so we can all gather our thoughts, then share?*
A few people are doing most of the talking.	*I'm noticing we're not hearing from everyone, so we're not getting the benefit of different perspectives. Let's go round-robin (and say "pass" if you prefer not to share).*
People are straying from the topic.	*Since we only have 10 minutes left and this is our chance to make a decision that impacts all of us, should we go back to the agenda and add the other topic to the parking lot?*
People are shooting down one another's ideas.	*It looks like some of us are coming up with ideas and some of us are evaluating them, so we're not making progress. Let's defer judgment for this meeting, then we can look at pros and cons of each idea next week.*
There is no clear decision maker or process.	*I'm realizing we don't have a clear process to make this decision, so we're not using our time well. How about we take 10 minutes to align on the DACI?*

Bonus: For meeting videos and a complete list of meeting course corrections, visit leaderlab.lifelabslearning.com.

***

Armed with the meeting tools and course-correcting prowess of great managers, Mia hits her Do-Over Button to return to her rocky meeting. Take a look at how she transforms an average meeting into an actual good use of her team's time:

Version 2: Do-Over

Mia:	Hey, everyone. As you know, we're decided to create client categories so we can better prioritize how we spend our time. So, the <u>purpose of this meeting is</u> to gather your ideas on criteria we should use to create these categories. <u>By the end of the meeting</u>, I'd like to have a list of at least 20 possible factors to consider. Then we can meet on Monday to narrow the list. Having these categories <u>will make all of our lives easier</u> since we'll have clear client service priorities and guidelines. <u>The process I'd like to follow today</u> is to silently jot down our ideas, share out loud, then open the floor to build on each other's ideas. Kofi will be the notetaker and Luca will be the timekeeper to keep us on track. How does that sound?
Kofi:	Sounds good.
Olivia:	I've been thinking an important factor is how many employees the company has. It's not just about how much they're spending but how much they can spend –

Mia:	Sorry to interrupt. <u>Looks like you already have ideas</u>, and I want to hear them, but I'd love to give everyone time to gather their thoughts <u>so we're all able to contribute well</u>. <u>How about we take three minutes now to jot down our thoughts in silence, then jump in to talk</u>?
Olivia:	Oh, right. Sorry. Got it.
	[After three minutes have passed]
Mia:	Okay, now that time's up, let's go round-robin one minute per person. Olivia, want to kick us off?
Olivia:	Yeah, so I just wrote down employees, industry, and past spend. Your turn, Luca.
Luca:	Is past spend all that helpful? What if they've used up their entire budget?
Kofi:	Well, that's not necessarily true. It depends on the timeline that we consider.
Mia:	Hm, <u>looks like we're starting to debate before getting all our ideas out there</u>, so <u>we might be limiting our options</u>. As a reminder, we'll meet on Monday to analyze the ideas and narrow the list. Today, the goal is to come up with a list of 20 ideas. <u>So, how about we defer judgment today and just try to capture as many ideas as possible</u>? Any ideas are welcome – even weird ones – in case they inspire us to think differently.
Luca:	Right good point. Okay, so, then my weird idea is to be able to see our client's bank accounts so we can tell how much money they have and use that as criteria. Kofi?
Kofi:	Actually, that makes me think one criteria could be how much funding the business has received and how recently. That's something we can even find out legally!

***

In summary: To improve your meetings faster, start with a *4P Opener*, use good tools, course-correct, and help your team do it too. Prevent meeting entanglement by clarifying if you are holding a meeting to Inform, Narrow, or Explore. To course-correct well, make a behavior observation, impact statement, and process suggestion. **Extract** your learnings often as a team through quick meeting retros to keep getting better.

🔦 MY LAB REPORT	Today's Date:
My takeaways:	
I regularly lead effective meetings:	1 2 3 4 5 6 7 8 9 10 (strongly disagree) strongly agree)
Experiment idea bank:	• If I have a meeting, then I'll start with the 4Ps. • If I notice entanglement, then I'll point it out. • If we go off track, then I will course-correct.
One small experiment I'll try to increase my score by 1 point:	
Post-experiment Learning Extractions:	

Bonus: Want to take your manager skills to the next level? Check out the bonus Inclusion Stations at leaderlab.lifelabs-learning.com.

My Learning Tracker

7 out of 7 Core BUs collected. 6 of 8 Core Skills collected.

Q-step	Playback	Deblur	Validate	Linkup	Pause	Extract
Coaching	Feedback	Productivity	1-on-1s	Strategic Thinking	Meetings Mastery	

14

Leading Change

Of all the difficult things a manager has to manage, change is one of the hardest. Increasingly, it is also one of the most common. So it makes sense that in our research, we found that great managers are unusually skilled at *leading change*. Some of these changes are massive – like helping a team handle a merger, a culture transformation, or a transition to remote work. Some changes are relatively small (but still challenging) – like rolling out a new technology, hiring or parting ways with a team member, or switching priorities. Some changes, like introducing a new process, are initiated by managers. And some changes, like a shift in company strategy, are determined by senior leaders, then executed by managers and their teams. All of these changes can result in meaningful success if led well, or turn out to be disasters when led poorly.

Consider a change initiative managed by Bernardo, one of the great managers we interviewed. When he was hired as a manager, he was one of the least tenured people at his company. Many people on his team had been there throughout half of their careers. They were comfortable in their roles and used to doing things a certain way. The company had enjoyed a long streak of success, but not long after Bernardo joined, it was suddenly at risk of being pushed out by a disruptive competitor. In an attempt to survive, corporate headquarters rolled out a new initiative, focused on fast and friendly customer service. Bernardo's team had to transition from providing customer support over the phone to instant chat. They had to learn new technology, respond in half the time, and come across as cheerful (despite feeling the exact opposite).

Throughout the company, productivity and engagement plummeted. Employees started quitting at record rates because of the stress they felt and the sudden disconnect from hearing voices over the phone to the impersonal experience of chat support. Bernardo also faced fear and resistance from his team members but, within one month, they became such a model of world-class service that they were asked to train employees in other regions. They weren't just great at the job; they were also more motivated by their work than they had been in a long time. At LifeLabs Learning, we wanted to operationalize the change leadership behaviors of great managers like Bernardo. Or, to put it less academically – we wanted to know how the heck they did it. How did they help their teams succeed and deal with the sobering fact that most change efforts are met with resistance (Blanchard et al. 2009)? To answer this question, we studied managers leading a wide range of change initiatives as well as executives specializing in leading company turnarounds – from organizational struggle to recovery. Throughout this chapter, we'll share what we learned so you can lead your team through changes of all shapes and sizes with even more confidence.

The Phases of Changes

The first thing we discovered by studying what great managers do differently is that they don't see change as a single event but rather as an ongoing process. Intuitively, they deduced a classic change-management model inspired by the writings of organizational psychologist Kurt Lewin (1947): Unfreeze, Change, Refreeze. To take your leading change skills to the next level, start by learning to recognize each phase. We'll get into each one in detail throughout this chapter, but let's start with a brief overview:

1. **Unfreeze:** "Thaw" people's habits and views so they soften to the possibility of change.
2. **Change:** Help people learn and apply new behaviors or ways of thinking.
3. **Refreeze:** "Solidify" into a new shape that represents the new normal.

To lead change well, first recognize the phase people are in. Next, select the right tool to use in each phase. While there are countless change tools, tips, and tricks, we'll help you master this skill faster by focusing on just the essentials. For each of the three phases, we will share two tools, equipping you with a six-point change map to lead any change more effectively.

Unfreeze Phase

Unfreeze	Change	Refreeze

When you look at the brain activity of people who are novices versus experts, you'll see a surprising difference between them. While the newbies' brains reveal a high degree of neural excitement, activating many different regions of the brain, the experts' brains are far quieter. They show less neural activity and more targeted activity in just a few parts of the brain (Kim et al. 2014). The same goes for anything else we do often. The more frequently we repeat a behavior, the more efficient and effortless it becomes. This neural tendency is great for saving time, but when it's time to change, neural comfort becomes a liability. In Lewin's terms, people who are used to acting and thinking in certain ways are "frozen" in these patterns. Before you can influence them to change, you have to help them "unfreeze."

A classic leadership mistake we see among average managers is rushing through the Unfreeze Phase or skipping it entirely. This is what happened across Bernardo's company in the example we shared at the start of this chapter. Most managers simply told people to do things differently. To their surprise, many team members pushed back or just kept doing things the old way. One of the things that made Bernardo's approach so unique was that he waited several weeks to roll out the changes. Paradoxically, to make the change stick faster, he **Paused** to hear his team's perspective and inspired them to try the new approach. Here's how:

Unfreeze Phase Tool #1: Hold a CAMPS Listening Tour

Remember the *CAMPS Model* we introduced in Chapter 11? It stands for **Certainty, Autonomy, Meaning, Progress,** and **Social** inclusion, and sums up the psychological brain cravings we all have that result in engagement. When leading change, great managers are especially attentive to people's *CAMPS* needs. To start "unfreezing" people from the status quo, they resist the urge to rush into change and **Pause** to hold what we call *CAMPS listening tours*. Instead of going into Telling Mode, they **Q-step** to investigate the impact of the change on people before rolling it out. And **Play back** what they hear. Take a look what happens in Mia's case when she skips this step with her manager, Alex:

Version 1

Mia: Hey Alex, I wanted to give you a heads-up that our team decided to create three different client categories. Moving forward, when you assign us a client, can you please also include their category using this rubric?

Alex: Wait, what? When did you start categorizing clients?

Mia: Oh, it's a new change we wanted to try out so we can dedicate the right amount of time to each type of client.

Alex: Okay, but we've already tried that, and it didn't work. And I already have a system in place for assigning clients. Why didn't you involve me early on? I could have told you that.

Mia: Oh! I'm sorry, Alex. I was just trying to make your life easier by figuring it out myself.

Which of Alex's *CAMPS* brain cravings are at stake? It's actually all of them. Below are questions that are probably swirling around in Alex's mind:

- **Certainty:** How does this new process work?
- **Autonomy:** Why is Mia telling me how to do my job? I'm her manager!
- **Meaning:** Why are we prioritizing this change now? Why does it matter?
- **Progress:** Is this going to slow me down? Will I have to throw away all the progress I made on our current system? Do they think the process I came up with is bad?
- **Social inclusion:** Why did they leave me out of this decision?

Great managers avoid springing change news on impacted stakeholders. They hold *CAMPS listening tours* by interviewing a diverse range of individuals to hear their thoughts, do **Playbacks** to show their understanding, and to signal that their perspectives count. This alone begins to "thaw" people's attachment to their current way of doing things. On their *listening tour*, they make sure to include people who:

- Will be impacted by the change
- Will feel strongly about it
- Might be vocal detractors
- Might be influential advocates
- Have to approve the change

A sample *CAMPS listening tour* invitation can read: "Within X months, we are planning to change Y because Z. I'm eager to hear your thoughts about it so we can find ways to roll it out as smoothly as possible." Be upfront about what aspects of the plan are fixed versus flexible. For example, "We are changing the logo because the new version received significantly more positive feedback from clients, but I want to hear your perspective before deciding on the right timeline and process." Once you get in the (physical or virtual) room, **Q-step** and **Playback** by using *CAMPS* as your guide.

Sample CAMPS listening tour questions:	
Overall	*What is your overall reaction to the change?*
Certainty	*What feels unclear or uncertain about it?* *What concerns do you have about it, if any?*
Autonomy	*What recommendations do you want us to consider?* *In which ways, if any, would you like to be involved?*
Meaning	*What about this change do you find exciting or important?* *How might you/your team help make it a success?*
Progress	*What can make this change at least 10% easier for you?* *Have you done any past work we can build on or learn from?*
Social inclusion	*Is there anyone else who might be impacted by the change?* *Who else do you think we should involve before making the change?*

If Mia had scheduled a *CAMPS listening tour* with Alex early on – when she first started contemplating the change – she could have earned Alex's buy-in faster and rolled out the change in a way that would make it more likely to stick. Seeing Alex's frustration, Mia turns to her Do-Over Button to go back in time:

Version 2: Do-Over

Mia: Hey Alex, the team and I have been thinking about creating different categories to streamline how we prioritize and support clients. <u>Before we start working on it, I was hoping to learn from your experience and hear your perspective. Can I ask you some questions</u>?

Alex: Sure. It's good that you're on the lookout for efficiency ideas. That said, we've tried it before, and it didn't work. Plus a lot of effort went into creating our current process.

Mia: Got it. Yeah. I definitely don't want to waste all that effort. My hope is to learn from the past and build on what we already have. <u>What do you think of the idea of creating categories</u>?

Alex: I can see it being valuable, but I've also seen it become way too complicated.

Mia: Yeah, I can see that. I'd really like to learn about what was tough about it. But, first, so I understand how you see it, can you tell me <u>what do you see as the biggest benefits</u>?

Alex: Well, I do think we can work smarter if we know who our high-potential clients are. We can also do better resource planning if we know how many of each type of client we have.

Mia: Good point. It sounds like efficiency and resource planning are important to consider. <u>How about any concerns you have</u>? You mentioned it got too complicated in the past.

Alex: Right. We ended up with too many categories, and it took so long to assign the categories that it wasn't worth it. Plus, we can miscategorize and miss out on a big opportunity.

Mia: Thanks for pointing that out. So, as we're thinking through solutions, we should make sure the process is lightweight and that it doesn't result in lost business. If we do that, <u>would you be open to considering some ideas to adjust our current process</u>?

Alex: Yeah, it doesn't hurt to look at it again with a fresh set of eyes.

Mia: Okay, great. And given your experience and the fact that your workflow would change if we roll out client categories, <u>how would you like to be involved</u>?

Alex: How about we schedule a meeting with you and your team so I can explain the history of what we've tried in the past? Then you all can come up with a plan and run it by me.

Thanks to these *CAMPS* questions (as well as the **Playback, Validation,** and **Linkup** BUs Mia uses throughout the conversation), Alex feels informed and included, and Mia and her team will get to **Extract** the learning from Alex's experience. Notice that Alex isn't convinced yet that the change is a good idea, but at the Unfreeze Phase, she doesn't have to be. What matters at this point is that Alex doesn't believe that Mia is trying to change her but rather that they are exploring the possibility of change together. Plus, instead of seeing Mia as a meddler, Alex will probably even come to see her as a strong strategic thinker.

Ironically, average managers avoid these types of conversations. They worry they will get pushback. But it is these very conversations that will make buy-in more likely later on. Keep in mind that the goal of **Pausing** to hold a *CAMPS listening tour* is not to convince people but to understand their reasoning. Instead of defending the plan, lean into your Core BUs. **Linkup** to explain why the change is worth considering. **Validate** and **Deblur** their concerns. **Extract** the learning from their past experiences. And if you find yourself getting defensive, **Pause** and **Q-step** to dig deeper, then **Play back** to fully understand their perspective.

Holding a *listening tour* will help you anticipate people's needs and improve your plan, but the chief reason this tool works so well in the Unfreeze Phase is that it gives people autonomy. There is a frequently repeated myth that humans dislike change. But look around. From new technology to new outfits, people are generally eager to explore, experiment, and make progress. The caveat? They have to feel in control of the change. As physician and change researcher Dean Ornish has been quoted in saying, "People don't resist change. They resist being changed" (Deutschman 2007).

Ornish saw this change management secret firsthand by observing his open-heart surgery patients. Even though he sent them home with strict guidelines to make lifestyle changes that would save their lives, few people made the simple changes he assigned, and many were even rushed back to the hospital again for repeat surgery. It was only once he began coaching patients to come up with their own solutions that he started seeing real change happen. Whether in an office or in the hospital, your biggest change opposition will almost always be the people you are trying to change. The less you *change them* and the more you *change with them*, the more likely you are to unfreeze their thinking early on, and the faster your change will succeed.

Unfreeze Phase Tool #2: Craft a Vision Statement

Your *CAMPS listening tour* should continue throughout the change process. Even after you implement your change, you'll want to check back in with people to help them adopt the new way of doing things, tweak your process based on their feedback, and keep signaling that their perspectives matter. But once you've completed the first round of your *listening tour*, you'll have insights to engineer your next Unfreeze Phase change tool: crafting a change *vision statement*.

A *vision statement* is a change "pitch" that you can use when you announce the change and share updates about it. If you learn that different stakeholders perceive the change differently, you may even need to craft different *vision statements* for different people, **Linking up** to what each cares about most. When speaking to a group of people, combine your *vision statements* to address their variety of concerns and earn support faster. So how do you engineer the right *vision statement*? Luckily, we have a formula to share with you (inspired by the great work of change researcher John Kotter) that will make it easier to choose the right things to say. Effective *vision statements* usually have the following four ingredients:

Validation	Heart	Head	Urgency
I realize that X will be a risk/ challenge . . .	*But imagine if . . . Consider the story of . . .*	*Research shows that . . . The numbers are . . .*	*We have to act now because . . .*

1. **Validation statement:** When average managers try to influence people to adopt a change, they tend to focus only on its positive aspects. The result? People are so distracted by the rebuttals in their minds that they hardly hear the positive message. What great managers do differently is **Validate** people's concerns up front. For example, "I realize that you are concerned about X. I am too," "It's true that there is a risk of Y," or "I know that this will take time and effort."

2. **Heart statement:** Once you've **Validated** people's concerns, your *vision statement* should speak to the "heart" – or more

literally, to people's emotions. Heart messages lean on feelings (especially pain, fear, empathy, excitement, and pride), metaphors, imagination, and story (especially centered on one individual). Emotions spur motion, so this is a vital ingredient. For example, "Imagine if X," "What if we could Y?" or "Consider the story of Z."

For an inspiring example of a heart statement profiled in the book *Switch* by Chip and Dan Heath (2010), take a look at an excerpt of a speech by Donald Berwick (2004), who set out to inspire hospitals to adopt a new patient safety protocol:

> *"The names of the patients whose lives we save can never be known. Our contribution will be what did not happen to them. And, though they are unknown, we will know that mothers and fathers are at graduations and weddings they would have missed, and that grandchildren will know grandparents they might never have known, and holidays will be taken, and work completed, and books read, and symphonies heard, and gardens tended that, without our work, would never have been."*

3. **Head statement:** Great managers also engage people's logic and reasoning. They share research, numbers, charts, and other concrete data. Even if people are emotionally bought-in, they'll need **Deblurred** information to help them rationalize their feelings and understand the reason for the change. For example: "Research shows that X," "We'll save Y money, or "We'll reduce time by Z%."

While Donald Berwick's heart statement was deeply moving, it wasn't sufficient to inspire people to unfreeze enough to make significant changes in their daily routines. Berwick and his team also added head statements to their pitch. They called their change initiative the "100,000 Lives campaign," and set out to save exactly 100,000 lives in 18 months. Their campaign slogan read: "Some is not a number. Soon is not a time."

4. **Urgency statement:** Skilled change leaders also add fuel to the fire. They **Deblur** why it's important to change now rather than wait to take action later. Focus on the risk or loss involved in waiting so that it's clear that inaction is also action. For example, "We have to act now because X," "If we wait any longer Y can happen," or "We have a rare opportunity now because Z."

Take a look at the *vision statement* Mia crafts for her change initiative for her next conversation with Alex:

Version 1: No Do-Over Needed

Mia: Thanks for meeting with me again to talk about the client categories project. I realize that categories didn't work well last time we tried and that trying again would take time and carry some risk. I'll consider those concerns carefully while exploring options. I'm eager to find the right solution to make sure our best clients, like Jen, don't have to sit around waiting for our replies and wondering if we care about them, while small clients drain our team's time, energy, and enthusiasm. Based on our calculations, the right process can save our team an average of 60 hours per month and increase annual revenue by 20%. The longer we wait to make a change, the more business we lose and the more we risk burning out our team.

Practice Station

A tough change one of the great managers we studied had to lead was helping her team adjust to their new company-wide policy of becoming entirely plant-based. Imagine you had to craft a *vision statement* to help your team embrace this change. Come up with your version before reading the sample below.

Validation	Heart	Head	Urgency
Sample: I realize many of you had your favorite foods to buy at work, and it feels bad to lose those options. But here's why I think this change is worth it –	We all believe in making this world better. What if we could make it better for animals too – animals just like Eva's pet pig, who is so loving and funny.	This year alone, we could save the lives of 3,000 animals, plus 45 million gallons of water, and reduce each person's carbon footprint from food by up to 73%.	If we make this change by next month, we would even be up for the Most Eco-Friendly Company award, which would get us great press attention.

Depending on the person, a better strategy might be to focus on saving the planet, becoming healthier, saving money, or coming across as innovative to others. Tailor your message to the person or share multiple *vision statements* when presenting to a group.

Now, think of a change you are leading or would like to lead. Create a first draft of your *vision statement*, using what you already know about your stakeholders:

Validation	Heart	Head	Urgency

Keep in mind that no matter how perfectly crafted your *vision statement* is, it won't be sufficient if the change requires ongoing action. The purpose of the *vision statement* is to inspire. The word "inspire" comes from the Latin *inspirare*, which means to breathe into. Think of inspiration as a breath of motivation. It might be enough to convince someone to take their first step, but it does not sustain change (just think of all those failed diet plans that start off with a burst of inspiration). But that's okay; the goal of the *vision statement* is simply to unfreeze people's thinking faster.

Change Phase

Unfreeze	Change	Refreeze

If you've handled the Unfreeze Phase well, you now understand your stakeholders' *CAMPS* needs, have made them feel heard, and have presented the change to them with a *vision statement* that speaks to their needs. You've reduced resistance and you have increased interest. Next, it's time to actually help people change their behavior. But, as we often say in psychology (thanks to neurobiologist, Carla Shatz), "cells that fire together, wire together." This means that our brains develop well-worn, efficient neural pathways for actions we repeat often. Changing our actions requires rewiring our brains.

If you've ever tried to change a habit, you know that this can be hard work. A helpful visual of the challenge with change is an adaptation of psychiatrist Elisabeth Kübler-Ross's Change Curve.

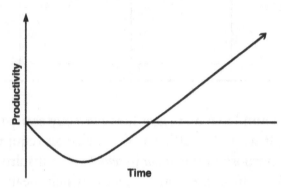

Source: LifeLabs Learning.

Notice that it is a J-curve, which means that *before* people can reap the benefits of the new way of doing things, they will first perform worse than when they were doing things the old way. It is when people leave their comfort zone and plummet down into the depths of that J that they are most frustrated by change. Researcher Rosabeth Moss Kanter has described this pit as Kanter's Law: "Everything looks like a failure in the middle." So how do great managers help people adopt change and accelerate up that J-curve faster? Here are our two favorite tools.

Change Phase Tool #1: Simplify the Plan

First, no matter how simple you think your change plan is now, *simplify the plan* even more. Think of all those poor brain circuits struggling to forge new neural pathways. Doing new things is effortful, and it can make people doubt their intelligence, which doesn't bode well for their eagerness to change. The best thing you can do to set people up for success is to make the change as cognitively lightweight as possible.

Bernardo, the manager who was responsible for helping his team transition to live chat support from phone support while following a new model of customer service, *simplified* his plan in several ways. First, he *removed* existing responsibilities where possible, including a report each team member had to create at the end of the day. Although these reports were not directly part of the change, his team now had additional time to learn and deal with that slowdown at the bottom of the J-curve. Next, he turned the new instructions his team members had to follow into a computer desktop image so they could have the information they needed immediately within reach. And throughout the first month, every time someone grumbled about the transition, he **Paused** to review the new process again. For more inspiration *simplifying* your change plans, here are some specific tactics we came across in our manager interviews:

- **Cut before adding.** Just as Bernardo did for his team, find something to cut, reduce, or pause before adding something new. Remember the J-curve. Change takes time. It doesn't just represent a new way of doing things – it represents additional effort.

- **Provide practice:** Remember that neurons that fire together, wire together. Create deliberate neuron wiring opportunities by holding practice sessions. Just as body-builders have to do "reps" (repetitions) to strengthen their muscles, skill builders need to get their reps in too. Set aside time for people to practice, **Q-step**, and get feedback.

- **Apply CAMPS listening tour insights:** Incorporate insights from your *listening tour* so that the plan feels as tailored to people's input as possible.

- **Use the Banana Principle:** Have you noticed that whenever there is a bowl of fruit in an office, the bananas almost always go first, while the oranges go last? Why are bananas so much more ap*peel*ing? Very simply, there is minimal friction between the desire to eat and the act of peeling. To make a new behavior more likely to happen, make it just a few seconds easier to start – like peeling a banana. To make an old behavior less likely to happen, make it just a few seconds harder to start – like peeling an orange. This is a change leadership hack Tania Luna and Jordan Cohen (2017) have nicknamed the Banana Principle. Psychologist Shawn Achor (2010) points out that just 20 seconds of "activation energy" can make all the difference. Want people to use a new webtool? Have them bookmark it. Want team members to stop interrupting one another with "quick questions"? Set a norm of wearing headphones when you need to concentrate. Want to encourage more collaboration? Preschedule coworking hours.

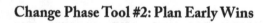

When in doubt about how to *simplify your plan*, extend your *listening tour* and **Q-step** with, "What would make this change at least 10% easier for you?" Remember to **Deblur** and **Playback** their answers.

Change Phase Tool #2: Plan Early Wins

Aside from *simplifying your plan*, how else can you help build momentum for change? One delightful way to do it is to **Pause** before the initiative even begins and plan an *early win*. Bernardo did this by assigning just three members of his team to handle chat support for two weeks. He collected customer praise, then asked his manager to hold a department-wide celebration. The pilot team members felt proud of their accomplishments and more excited to be part of the change. What's more, they became the "poster kids" of the change company-wide.

Nearly all of the best change leaders we studied spoke about the importance of creating *early, visible wins*. Why? Early successes boost confidence, release dopamine, and become tangible representations of the value of the change. They make that top of the J-curve visible and seem within reach. Without *early wins*, the journey to change can feel like a relentless uphill climb.

Practice Station
Take a moment now and think back to the change you are leading or would like to lead. What is a small, early win you can already plan now? How will you promote it?

Refreeze Phase

Unfreeze	Change	**Refreeze**

At this point you've unfrozen people and helped them start making change. Once people start to adopt new behaviors, it can be easy to assume that the change initiative is over. In most cases though, leaders don't do enough to help their teams "refreeze" into the desired new shape. Early enthusiasm wears off, everyone spends less time focused on the change initiative, and people slide back to their old comfort zones. A common version of this phenomenon is the notorious New Year's resolution. For example, people vow to work out more often, spend most of January at the gym, then life gets in the way throughout the rest of the year. How do great managers help change stick more quickly and sustainably? Here are two tools they use.

Refreeze Phase Tool #1: Overcommunicate

Some changes are entirely involuntary. Gmail changes versions again. A pandemic sweeps the globe, making billions of people work from home. But most changes require ongoing reminders for behaviors to truly refreeze. Great managers recognize this and don't just communicate about the change in the beginning but intentionally *overcommunicate* on an ongoing basis. In other words, they talk about the change even more often than they think they need to – but not to the point of repeating the message so much that people tune out. How do you find that right balance?

In the world of advertising, the question of how many times a message should be repeated before it sticks is called "effective frequency," a term popularized by Michale Naples (1979). Just how frequent does a message have to be to become effective? A meta-analysis of research has found a range of 10 to 20 repetitions to be optimal (Bornstein 1989). It turns out we also tend to like messages we hear more often (Fang, Singh, and Ahluwalia 2007), and managers who repeat their messages are more likely to help their team members deliver work on time and budget (Leonardi et al. 2011).

But here's the trick: the most effective managers keep their repetitive communication feeling fresh. They recruit multiple spokespeople aside from themselves, they use diverse channels (like email, group meetings, one-on-one conversations, videos, and even balloons and bathroom posters), and they space out their messages into communication "drip campaigns." Just as there is no consensus in the advertising world on how many repetitions it takes to convert a browser into a buyer, there is no one right way to *overcommunicate*. So do it often, do it in many different ways, and do it just a little more than you think you need. If people seem to forget your message, don't take it personally. Remember that leaders have to help people create new neural pathways.

Refreeze Phase Tool #2: Create Behavioral Cues

While reminding people of change is important, great managers do more to help new behaviors refreeze. They leverage their team's environments to create *behavioral cues*. Unlike a reminder, which keeps a message top of mind but not necessarily at the most relevant moments, a behavioral cue prompts the target behavior just when it needs to happen. In this way, you are not relying on people's memories but on what behavioral economists Cass Sunstein and Richard Thaler (2009) have famously dubbed "nudges." Here are a few of our favorite examples:

- **Link to existing habits.** Use the power of *if-thens* (from Chapter 9). Is there an existing habit or process that your team is already familiar with? Find ways to "link" the new behavior to the existing one. For example, if you want to strengthen your team's feedback culture and you already have weekly one-on-ones, build a feedback prompt into the agenda (if we're in a one-on-one meeting, then we'll exchange feedback). If you want to change your expense tracking system and your team members already submit time sheets, create a cue to attach receipts along with time sheets.

- **Create a checklist.** One of the best ways to help people remember to do something is to eliminate the need to remember it. Create – or, better yet, co-create – a checklist instead. As the surgeon Atul Gawande illustrates in his book *The Checklist Manifesto* (2009), checklists save lives across multiple industries, from medicine to aviation.

- **Establish feedback loops:** Rather than give feedback every time you see someone do (or not do) the new behaviors, build ongoing feedback loops into your team's environment. For example, aside from having to switch to live chat support, Bernardo's team was also expected to use a new, more customer-centric service model. Bernardo asked his team members to come up with ideas to help the change stick and, together, they agreed to two feedback loops: (1) a weekly self-assessment "pop quiz" each person would **Pause** to take, and (2) a monthly peer shadowing ritual where team members reviewed one another's chat logs and shared feedback using a checklist.

To create *behavioral cues* for your change initiative, ask yourself: "When will people have the choice of doing things the old way or the new way?" "What kind of prompt can cue the right behavior at the right time?" and "How can I embed cues that prompt that right behavior even when I'm not around?" For even more buy-in, leverage the power of autonomy. Develop your *behavioral cues* together with the people who will be using them. And for best results, **Pause** from time to time to **Extract** your learnings and improve your feedback loops.

Stay Slushy

The Unfreeze → Change → Refreeze model simplifies the complexity of change, making it easier for managers to develop their change skills faster. But there's just one caveat: when change is constant, we must not refreeze too rigidly. In fact, Lewin pointed this out even back in the 1940s, referring to change as a continual process of adaptation (1947). By reviewing his past writing, researchers Stephen Cummings and team realized that Lewin likely never even used the term "refreeze" (Cummings, Bridgman, and Brown 2015).

So, we would hereby like to introduce a slight amendment to the change model that we think Kurt Lewin would approve:

Unfreeze	*Change*	*Stay Slushy*

The best managers we studied didn't just lead one or two change initiatives. Sure, some changes were bigger than others, but small changes happened all the time. In fact, treating change as a rare, finite, and finished process is a quick way to set people up for stress and disappointment.

Instead, great managers help their teams stay slushy: just solid enough for new behaviors to take hold but not so frozen that they can't quickly adapt. How do these managers strike that balance? They regularly *normalize change* and *make change normal*.

Normalize Change

From day one, great managers let their team members know that processes and policies are all works in progress and that they will continue to evolve – ideally with the team's help. These managers often refer to change initiatives as "experiments" to invite a mindset of curiosity and encourage **Extracting** learning. And when change feels hard, they **Validate** people's feelings, acknowledging that their reactions are normal, and helping them focus on the benefits of change. In short, instead of treating change as rare and people's reactions to change as unusual, they *normalize change* so that it feels less threatening and more exciting.

Once Mia finds out that the rumored merger at her company is going through after all, she meets with her team – crafting a *vision statement* based on the *CAMPS listening tour* she started when she learned about the possibility of a merger. Notice how she normalizes the change:

Version 1: No Do-Over Needed

Mia: I have some news about the merger we've all been wondering about. I just learned it's going through next month. <u>I realize this brings up lots of questions and concerns</u>, but I am really excited about the opportunity this creates for us. Imagine how much faster we'll be able to do our work with the other company's technology. It will feel like getting a rocket strapped to our backs. Their tech will save us 10 hours a week *each*. The faster we make this transition work well, the faster we can stop doing manual calculations and get started on some of the dream projects we've had to keep on hold. I don't have any other information yet, but I wanted to create space for us to just process the news together. *[Pause.]*

Luca: I figured this would happen.

Kofi: It's pretty unnerving honestly. I just got here.

Olivia: It's pretty unnerving for us too. We have our systems all figured out. I bet we're going to have to change our entire workflow now.

Luca: If we even keep our jobs. Maybe their tech is so good they won't need us.

Mia: We don't have any reason to doubt our job security right now, but <u>you're right that we should expect things to change. Change is hard, and yeah, it will slow us down at first,</u> but I do think it will improve how we work and create new learning and career opportunities. Plus, <u>it's our chance to make other changes we've been wanting.</u> Are

> there aspects of the merger you all are excited about? *[Pause]*
>
> **Kofi:** Well, I did always want to work at a larger company. Looks like this is my chance.
>
> **Olivia:** I agree that the tech is exciting. I'm so sick of calculating everything by hand.
>
> **Luca:** Yeah . . . I'm cautiously optimistic about the tech and getting to develop new skills.
>
> **Mia:** Same for me. <u>I'm feeling nervous-excited, and we'll probably all feel that way for the next few months. Let's keep reminding each other it's normal.</u> And if you ever want to talk through your reaction one-on-one, I'm always happy to do that.

Keep Change Normal

So, we know that great managers handle change well when it happens and normalize the change, but they also help their teams stay slushy by *keeping change normal*. Instead of letting team members get too cozy in their comfort zones and become too frozen in their ways, the best leaders create change on a regular basis. Following are some of our favorite examples:

- Hold quarterly retros (see Chapter 10) to share feedback, **Extract** learnings, and come up with improvements the team can make.
- Rotate meeting roles (see Chapter 13) to create a sense of novelty.
- Help each person create an individual development plan to collect new skills. (We'll delve further into this practice in the next chapter.)

- Teach one another something new every month.
- Read a new book together once a quarter.
- Invite a client, instructor, or member of another team once a quarter.
- Shadow other team members to learn tips and tricks from one another.
- Pick one process or system to improve once a quarter.
- Nudge people to take risks and actively stretch their zone of comfort.
- Call out and celebrate people's adaptivity and flexibility whenever they see it.

In summary: To lead change well, recognize that change is a process: unfreeze → change → refreeze (but stay slushy). Hold *CAMPS listening tours, craft a vision statement, simplify, plan early wins, overcommunicate, create behavioral cues, normalize change,* and *keep it normal.*

☀️ MY LAB REPORT	Today's Date:
My takeaways:	
I regularly introduce small changes:	1 2 3 4 5 6 7 8 9 10 (strongly disagree) (strongly agree)
Experiment idea bank:	▪ If a change is coming up, then I will schedule a CAMPS listening tour. ▪ If I want people to change, then I will create at least 10 reminders or cues. ▪ If my team hasn't felt change in a while, then I'll suggest learning something new.

One small experiment I'll try to increase my score by 1 point:	
Post-experiment Learning Extractions:	

Bonus: Want to take your manager skills to the next level? Check out the bonus Inclusion Stations at leaderlab.lifelabs-learning.com.

My Learning Tracker

7 out of 7 Core BUs collected. 7 of 8 Core Skills collected.

Q-step	Playback	Deblur	Validate	Linkup	Pause	Extract
Coaching	Feedback	Productivity	1-on-1s	Strategic Thinking	Meetings Mastery	Leading Change

15

People Development

Based on a global study of nearly three million employees across 54 industries, two of the best predictors of employee engagement are positive responses to the following (Harter et al. 2020):

- "There is someone at work who encourages my development."
- "In the past year, I have had opportunities at work to learn and grow."

Pause and consider: how do you think each person on your team would respond? How about when it comes to their perception of the future? How satisfied are they with their future career growth opportunities at your company? In another large-scale global study, 70% of employees reported being dissatisfied with their opportunities for career advancement. But here's the fascinating paradox: the same study found that 75% of executives surveyed expected to face a *shortage* of skills and knowledge among their employees (CEB 2015). To summarize:

- A sense of development is essential to engagement (and thus productivity and retention).
- Employees believe there aren't enough opportunities to grow.
- Employers believe that employees aren't growing fast enough!

Within this gap is a bright and shining leadership opportunity just waiting to emerge. But most employees and managers aren't sure where to begin. After all, career paths are becoming increasingly curvy and nonlinear, looking less like ladders and more like rock climbing walls. It's rare (if not impossible) these days to lay out a predictable path toward that next rung on the career ladder. This reality spells more uncertainty, but it also means that people have more opportunities to tailor their career paths to meet their unique strengths, interests, and life priorities. So, how do great managers help their team members find those paths and grow faster?

If you are coaching, giving feedback, enabling productivity, holding effective one-on-ones, and helping people think strategically – you are already way ahead of the game. These Core Skills transform nearly all your team member interactions into development opportunities. And you aren't just helping people do good work today; you are building their capacity to take on more responsibilities in the future. But thanks to our research, we found that great managers have one other unique skill that helps them accelerate their team's growth. We refer to this skill as *people development*. It consists of knowing how to (1) identify business needs, (2) identify individual needs, (3) help people develop high leverage skills, and (4) make development a theme rather than a rare event. Throughout this chapter, we'll share how to develop each of these capabilities faster so you can help your team members grow and so you can maximize your own development deliberately.

Identify Business Needs: Capability Mapping

Let's begin with a quick visit to Mia and Luca to see a common career conversation in action:

Version 1

Mia:	I was hoping to check back in on the career growth conversation we started in our last one-on-one. How have you been feeling about it since then?

Luca: Okay . . . not great, to be honest. I still don't feel like I'm growing much or getting anywhere new professionally.

Mia: I thought you said you wanted to focus on project management. No?

Luca: Yeah, I know. But I don't really feel like I'm learning anything. Maybe I should pick a different focus.

Mia: Okay, yeah. What would be interesting to learn?

Luca: I don't know. Maybe web design is worth looking into again. I've been curious about it.

Mia: I can see you being good at that. Maybe look into some online classes.

Luca: Yeah. There are a lot of those out there.

Mia: Yep. That sounds like a plan. Let me know how it goes!

Luca isn't sure what development areas to prioritize, and Mia isn't sure how to help him figure it out. What's more, Mia is making a common but unfortunate leadership mistake. She hasn't taken the time to **Pause** and **Deblur** which skills are most needed on her team and the business at large, so she can't help Luca differentiate between development opportunities that are must-have versus nice-to-have. When we studied great managers, this was the first thing we noticed them do to think strategically about their team members' development and the capabilities most needed on their team. In particular, they made it their job to be able to answer these two questions:

1. **Current state:** Where do we need more knowledge, skills, or experience as a team? *(Consider where your team needs more backup in case someone is out or leaves and what projects you can't start or delegate because of a capability gap on the team.)*

2. **Future state:** What skills, knowledge, and experience will our team need in 1–2 years? *(Consider new challenges that might arise and new opportunities on the horizon.)*

Equipped with this information, you can make and share a *capability map*, so that everyone on your team is aware of the highest-priority development opportunities.

Practice Station

Create a first draft of a *capability map* for your team. In the column on the right, jot down the skill, knowledge, and experience areas your team most needs. Circle the top priorities:

Current state: What knowledge, skills, or experiences would help your team achieve current goals faster and create backup?	*Sample: managing large accounts, X software*
Future state: What skills, knowledge, and experiences will your team need in 1–2 years to achieve your goals or reduce risk?	*Sample: leading change, statistical analysis*

In essence, a *capability map* is a *gap analysis* (see Chapter 12). It prompts you to **Deblur** your goals and work backwards to identify capability gaps. In some cases, it will be easy to identify the gaps on your own. In other cases, you'll need to collaborate with your team, manager, and other leaders within and outside of your organization. For example, if you expect that your team will double in size in the next 12 months but don't have enough experience to anticipate what skills this change will require, interview others who have gone through a similar transition and **Q-step**: "Knowing what you know now, what skills or knowledge do you believe we need to start building now to be able to reach this goal in the future?"

After her initial conversation with Luca, Mia decides to speak with her manager about the department's current and future people development needs. Armed with fresh insights from the discussion, Mia hits the Do-Over Button and goes back in time to speak with Luca again:

Version 2: Do-Over
Mia: I was hoping to check back in on the career growth conversation we started in our last one-one-one. How have you been feeling about it since then?
Luca: Okay . . . not great, to be honest. I still don't feel like I'm growing much or getting anywhere new professionally.
Mia: I'm sorry to hear that. Just to check: are you still seeing "professional development" as building new skills?
Luca: Yeah. That's what I feel like I'm most missing lately.

> **Mia:** Okay. <u>So that we can think about this strategically, would it be helpful if I shared some of the skills that are most needed in the department?</u>
>
> **Luca:** Yes, please. That would be really helpful.

When sharing their *capability map*, some managers we interviewed focused primarily on the development opportunities on their team. Others focused on the organization as a whole, with the aim of helping team members grow and contribute, even if it meant eventually changing roles and leaving their team. Surprisingly, when managers helped their team members think of their development within *and* beyond the scope of their role (and even beyond their company), their team members were more likely to be engaged by their current work and less likely to leave.

Identify Individual Needs: The Zoom Out Conversation

So, to help their team members develop faster, great managers first identify the most important development needs on a business level. Another way of thinking about this is to imagine the *capability gap* as demand in the marketplace. This is what the business is willing and eager to pay people to do, provided they have the necessary skills and knowledge. But this information alone misses what your team members are willing and eager to supply. For example, even though there might be tremendous demand for public speaking skills in your department, it doesn't mean that anyone on your team will want to develop their public speaking skills. Great managers make it a habit to regularly **Linkup** to business needs and *individual development needs*. In this way, they can help each team member find the workplace equivalent of "product-market-fit." In other words, they make it easier for others to find that sweet spot between what they want to get better at and what they can get paid to do.

How can you identify and help your team members identify their development needs? One tool we share with managers in our workshops at LifeLabs Learning is what we call a *Zoom Out Guide*. This is an opportunity to **Pause** and zoom out to see the big picture rather than staying hyper-focused on daily tasks. Schedule time to **Q-step** by asking your team members these *Zoom Out* questions at least once or twice a year, and **Play back** what you hear:

Zoom Out Guide	
Loves and loathes	What types of work do you want to do more of, less of, and why?
Strengths	What do you see as your biggest strengths? How often do you use them?
Energizers	What challenges or goals excite you or matter to you most and why?
No-go list	What types of work are you pretty sure you do *not* want to do?
Priorities	What are your career priorities (for example, more responsibility, using strengths and energizers more, more pay, more flexibility, less stress)?
Role models	Whose work do you admire or are you curious to learn more about?
Mastery	In what ways can you become even more effective in your current role?
Goals	What responsibilities or roles might you want to take on in 1–5 years?
Gaps	What might hold you back from attaining your goals?

Capabilities	Let's **Extract** the learning: what skills, knowledge, or experiences might help you do more of the work you want and achieve your career priorities?

 Bonus: For developmental coaching videos and a *Zoom Out Guide* template, visit leaderlab.lifelabslearning.com.

***

Sometimes you and your team members will have all the information you need to answer these *Zoom Out* questions together. In other cases, the *Zoom Out Guide* might serve as a nudge to **Deblur** goals or collect information from others. For example, to better understand personal gaps, you can encourage your team members to pull for feedback from others (see Chapter 9). And to identify gaps for roles that aren't within your realm of expertise, encourage interviewing others. Though it's tempting for managers to take on all mentoring responsibilities themselves, research shows that managers who are best at developing others connect their team members to other subject matter experts (Gartner 2018).

Practice Station

Pop quiz! Pick one of your team members and answer each of the following questions about them:

- Which of their tasks or responsibilities do they enjoy most?

• In what area(s) do they most crave feedback?

• What are their career priorities?

Check in with them in your next one-on-ones to see if you were right.

Sometimes your team members won't know how to answer all of the *Zoom Out* questions. Increasingly, we hear from managers in our workshops that people tell them they don't know what they want to do. The options appear to be limitless and the details of various career paths are mysterious. How does one choose or even know where to begin?

If this is the case with people on your team, first **Validate** that challenge. Given the rock climbing shape of so many companies today, more and more people don't know "what they want to be when they grow up" (the authors of this book proudly included). Normalize this reality with your team, and point out that career growth is less about linear progress and more about exploring options, developing relationships, and collecting transferable skills and knowledge. Success in this ecosystem means having a diversified portfolio of capabilities that makes it possible to be increasingly "employable" in a wide range of roles.

While it can be freeing to have many options, it can also keep us from taking action (Schwartz 2004). So it's essential to encourage folks to simply start somewhere. Help your team members conduct small experiments by learning new things, taking on new assignments, and learning from others about their work. After every new experience, help them **Extract** their learnings about what kind of work they like and – just as importantly – what they don't like, and use lots of **Playbacks** to help them reflect. The goal here is not to find that one perfect role but to become increasingly self-aware about what type of work is most meaningful, energizing, and suited to one's individual needs.

High Leverage Development: Get in the Venn Zone

With an understanding of business needs and individual needs, managers can see the overlay of supply and demand and show their team members the highest leverage opportunities for development. Think of this as the *MIT* development opportunities. We call the beautiful center space where people's personal growth needs align with business needs the *"Venn Zone."*

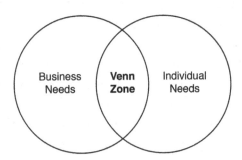

Source: LifeLabs Learning.

Helping people get in the *Venn Zone* propels the fastest development because resources to support individual growth exist in this space. People can take on real-world challenges and learn by doing. New roles and responsibilities are also most likely to dwell in the *Venn Zone*. But what happens when a development need lives outside the *Venn Zone*? This is also helpful information for managers to have. You can handle these gaps in the following ways.

Individual Needs Mismatch: Recruit

If the business has needs that do not overlap with individual development needs, it is likely a prompt to hire or look for help outside of the organization.

Business Needs Mismatch: Deblur Expectations.

If individual development needs do not **Linkup** to business needs, this is a prompt to set expectations. Here is a silly (though not altogether unrealistic) example:

> *"Just so we're aligned: I don't expect cooking skills to become a priority since we're a tech company. Let me know if you'd like to explore other development opportunities you'll be more likely to use at work. That said – if you want to keep building your cooking skills for fun, you are more than welcome to cater our team lunches!"*

Keep in mind that while there may not be a current business need or even an anticipated business need, the future is very good at surprising us. Many innovative companies deliberately carve out time for employees to take on projects and develop skills that seem irrelevant to the business. Least of all, this practice builds engagement, a love of learning, and *slushiness* (see Chapter 14) and, best of all, it creates new business opportunities. As a case in point, Google's Gmail started out as a passion project.

Missing Capability: Have a Gap Conversation

Another tricky mismatch that managers face is when a development opportunity (like a role or a responsibility) exists and does align with a team member's needs but not with their current capability. If the costs of learning by doing are relatively low, it's usually worth it to give people a chance. If the costs or risks are high, the best course of action is usually a "gap conversation." For example:

> *"Here are the requirements for this opportunity . . .. Here are areas where I see a fit and where I see a gap . . .. While I can't guarantee that you'll get this opportunity, I want to support you in making it as likely as possible, whether now or in the future. With that in mind, would you like to work together to close that gap?"*

Individual Development Plans and 3Es

Once you've identified each person's *Venn Zone* opportunities, don't let them go the way of the New Year's resolution. The next step to help people develop faster is turning ideas into action. Here's how.

Individual Development Plan (IDP)

Nearly every great manager we studied encouraged their team members to create some form of an *Individual Development Plan (IDP)*. An *IDP* is a written commitment to focus on a specific development area for a specific period of time. The more **Deblurred** it is, the more likely people are to follow through. Here is a template we share with our workshop participants:

INDIVIDUAL DEVELOPMENT PLAN	SAMPLE ANSWERS
Capability: What is the development area?	*Communication skills*
Linkup: Why is it important to you to develop in this area? *(How will it help you and others?)*	*I'll help build more alignment on our team. Communication skills will also help me with my goal of taking on a leadership role.*

INDIVIDUAL DEVELOPMENT PLAN	SAMPLE ANSWERS
Focus: What's a specific BU, skill, or knowledge area you want to grow?	*Playbacks and split-tracks*
Self-assessment: What is your current capability level on a scale of 1–10?	*6*
Manager assessment: What is your manager's assessment of your level on a scale of 1–10?	*7*
Success criteria: How would a 10 look?	*Using playbacks and split-tracks in most one-on-one and team conversations*
3E ideas to increase your score by 1 point: *[Note: we'll explain what this means in the section below]*	
Education (book, article, podcast, class)	*Read* The Leader Lab
Experience (projects, practice)	*Give myself a point for each playback I do*
Exposure (interview, shadow)	*Observe how Dean does this in meetings*
Next steps: What (specifically) will you do? Pick ideas from the 3E idea bank.	*Read* The Leader Lab*!*
Timeline: When will you do it?	*Start tomorrow, finish one month from today.*
Check points: When and how will we check in about it?	*I will put it on our one-on-one agenda one month from now.*

Bonus: Download an *IDP* template at leaderlab.lifelabs-learning.com.

***

This version of an *IDP* helps people start with a broad capability (for example, communication skills, graphic design, public speaking, decision making, learning a programming language, strategic thinking, influence skills). This can be someone's development area for 6, 12, or even 24 months. Help create motivation by **Linking up** the development goal to outcomes that are personally meaningful. Then help people pick a narrower focus every one to three months. Think back to the manager research we conducted at LifeLabs Learning. While listening skills are a broad capability, the specific BUs required to master it might include letting people finish their thoughts, staying attentive, and doing **Playbacks**. **Deblur** and break down the broad capability into these small components to help people develop faster.

To provide support and positive pressure for your team members to stay on track, build in **Pause** points in your one-on-ones to celebrate wins, **Validate** and cheer on their struggles, **Extract** learnings, and decide on new focus areas. Encourage small, steady progress, by **Q-stepping** with, "What will help you improve by just one point on a scale of one to 10?" The more deliberate and consistent your development conversations are, the more rapid progress people will make.

3E Model

Once you've helped each person on your team identify their development focus, how can you help them generate ideas to build this competency? In the sample *IDP* above, you may have noticed a prompt to come up with *3E* ideas. The *3E Model* is a framework that sparks ideas for development. The *3Es* stand for:

1. **Education:** Learn by acquiring new information. For example, read a book, take a class, listen to a podcast, attend a conference, subscribe to a newsletter, watch a video, read research,

get certified. Pro-tip: To help people get the most of their education, leverage the protégé effect, which we mentioned at the start of this book. People learn faster by teaching, so create opportunities to share summaries and teach others on the team (Chase et al. 2009).

2. **Experience:** Learn by doing. For example, volunteer, mentor someone, join a task force, build a business case for a new idea or role, offer to help people with their work, take on a new assignment, set a challenging goal. Pro-tip: While experience is a good teacher, it can be easy to forget that it's a learning opportunity, which results in what we call "experience float." To help people **Extract** the learning from their experience, **Pause** and demarcate it. For example, "Wow. You just did that for the first time. What did you learn?"

3. **Exposure to role models:** Learn by observing others. For example, shadow someone's work, pull for feedback, ask for advice, ask interview questions. This final E of the *3E Model* is often the least used but also the most important. According to the famous learning psychologist Albert Bandura, we humans learn best through observation, imitation, and modeling. Pro-tip: Support your team members in leveraging this E, helping them create interview questions and making introductions.

Bonus: For a list of our favorite *3E* recommendations, visit leaderlab.lifelabslearning.com.

***

The *3E Model* is a great reminder that there are not just many different things to learn but also many different *ways* to learn. Ask your team members how they prefer to learn and encourage mixing up the Es. If someone on your team is struggling to set development goals, the *3E Model* is also a handy framework to encourage experimentation. With the *IDP* and *3E* tools in mind, let's join Mia for one final conversation with Luca:

Version 2: Do-Over (Continued)

Mia: Okay, so it sounds like we both think that the <u>highest-leverage development area</u> for you right now is still project management.

Luca: Right. But with a focus on cross-functional project management, which is the part I think I was missing before.

Mia: Yes, great. <u>What is it about this development focus that's important to you?</u>

Luca: Well, I care a lot about improving our processes, as you know. With the merger coming up, I think I can be the go-to for cross-functional process improvements if it's an area I'm strong in.

Mia: Agreed! <u>So, let's break it down. What is one specific aspect of cross-functional project management skills you can focus on first?</u>

Luca: I was thinking I can get better at influencing people when I don't have formal authority.

Mia: <u>Okay, and what's a specific skill or knowledge area that would help you get better at that this month?</u>

Luca: Probably the best place to start would be learning terminology people use in different departments, including at the new company, so I can speak their language.

Mia: I love that. <u>Which department would be a good place to start?</u>

Luca: I'd be curious to start with engineering.

Mia: <u>And on a scale of 1–10, how would you rate your current level of engineering terminology knowledge</u>?

Luca: Hmm. I'd give myself a 5 right now. What do you think?

Mia: Nice. I agree based on what I've seen. <u>And how would a 10 look</u>?

Luca: Well, I don't need to be an actual expert in programming languages, so for me a 10 would be sitting in on an engineering meeting and understanding what they're talking about.

Mia: Yeah, that would be a good test. <u>Let's chat about some ideas for how to get there. What education, experience, or exposure opportunities come to mind for you</u>?

Luca: Well, I can subscribe to engineering blogs or even take an online class. I can also ask to see their goals for the quarter and look up what all the terms mean. What do you think?

Mia: Yeah, I like that. The other thought that comes to mind for me is to actually see if you can already sit in on some meetings, then jot down the unfamiliar terms and ask people to explain them after the meeting.

Luca: Oh, I like that. I can see if Alyssa would be fine with me sitting in on the engineering team meetings this month. Then throughout the month, I can build my own glossary.

Mia: Great. <u>I'll jot that down in your IDP. How would you want to check in throughout the month to stay on track</u>?

Luca: How about in each one-on-one, I share what terms I learned that week?

Make Development a Theme

To recap, great managers help people develop faster by sharing business needs, helping their team members articulate their development using **Q-steps** and **Playbacks**, identifying the *Venn Zone* of high leverage development opportunities, and encouraging deliberate development using an *IDP*. But there is one more habit of great managers we noticed in our research: they *make development a theme*. In other words, they don't treat growth and learning as occasional events but rather as a constant way of thinking and being at work.

Set Development Expectations

For starters, great managers make it clear that while their role is to provide support, each person on their team is responsible for their own development. They are the drivers of their growth rather than passive passengers, waiting for someone to come "grow them." By setting this expectation up front, managers empower their teams to prioritize their growth and keep exploring opportunities. A sample expectation-setting message might be:

> *"I'm here for you to help you grow in ways that are most meaningful to you and help our team succeed, but ultimately you'll know best what you need. People who do well here are proactive about their own development. They find ways to stretch their skills, contribute, develop new relationships, and pull for feedback often. Whenever you want to experiment with new ways to grow or if you just want an accountability partner, don't hesitate to come to me for support."*

Create a Cadence

Another way managers set up their teams for development success is to encourage a predictable cadence of **Pausing** to focus on learning **Extractions** and goal-setting. For example, schedule a *Zoom Out* conversation twice a year, an *IDP* review every quarter, and a brief development check-in weekly in your one-on-one meetings. Ask:

- "Last week you said you wanted to do _____ as a small step. How did it go?"
- "What did you learn?"
- "What's something small you will try next week?"

Demarcate and Track

In the introduction to this book ("The Backstory") we mentioned Niko, a great manager we studied who helped her team members update their résumés every year on their work anniversaries. Though it was a controversial move, her team had some of the best retention rates in the company. Not only did Niko create a cadence, the other aspect of this ritual that worked so well was that she helped her team members **Pause** to *demarcate and track* their progress.

Even when people learn a great deal, their progress can be invisible to them. In school, we used exam scores, moving up grades, and graduating as markers of growth. At work – especially in relatively flat companies with few titles – it can be difficult to recognize advancement. Many of the great managers we studied came up with ways to make people's development visible. They *demarcated* new skills, knowledge, experiences, goals reached, and confidence levels earned by calling them out one-on-one, **Linking up** to their development goals, and celebrating as a group. Many also encouraged *tracking* these progress markers, whether by updating their résumés or creating a portfolio of accomplishments. It turns out people develop even faster when they see evidence of their past development.

Bonus: Download a development tracker template at leaderlab.lifelabslearning.com.

***

In summary: To help people develop faster, identify business needs, hold Zoom Out conversations to understand individual needs, and use *IDPs* and *3Es* (Education, Experience, Exposure) to help people make progress in the *Venn Zone*. To make development a theme, set expectations, create a cadence, and help people demarcate and track progress.

MY LAB REPORT	**Today's Date:**
My takeaways:	
I regularly have development conversations with my team members:	1 2 3 4 5 6 7 8 9 10 (strongly disagree) (strongly agree)
Experiment idea bank:	▪ If someone makes progress, then I will demarcate it by calling it out. ▪ If someone wants more career growth, then I will ask what career growth means to them. ▪ If someone isn't sure how to develop, then I will suggest doing 3E experiments.
One small experiment I'll try to increase my score by 1 point:	
Post-experiment Learning Extractions:	

Bonus: Want to take your manager skills to the next level? Check out the bonus Inclusion Stations at leaderlab.lifelabs-learning.com.

My Learning Tracker

7 out of 7 Core BUs collected. 8 of 8 Core Skills collected.

Q-step	Playback	Deblur	Vali-date	Linkup	Pause	Extract	
Coaching	Feedback	Produc-tivity	1-on-1s	Strategic Thinking	Meetings Mastery	Leading Change	People Develop-ment

Leader Lab Wrap-up

In the last chapter, we spoke about the importance of acknowledging and demarcating progress. So, let's do it! You've now reached the final chapter of this book, and it's time to celebrate. Let's first reflect on all the BUs, skills, and tools you've collected, briefly check in with Mia the Manager, then finally, re-test your leadership skills so you can see how far you've come.

Core BUs, Skills, and Tools at a Glance

Do a quick scan of each of the Behavioral Units, skills, and tools you've added to your manager toolbox. Quiz yourself to see if you remember them and consider how you've applied each one:

Core Behavioral Units						
Q-step	Playback	Deblur	Validate	Linkup	Pause	Extract
Core skills and tools						
Coaching	*SOON Funnel*					
Feedback	*Q-BIQ Method, Feedback Salsa*					
Productivity	*Time language, stop/start meetings on time, time audit, MITs, Quadrants, Buckets, CCS, Closed Loop Culture, If-thens, Pomodoro, Kanban*					
One-on-Ones	*CAMPS Model*					
Strategy	*Gap analysis, 3 Lenses Model, UC Check, Inclusive Planning*					

Meetings	4P Opener, q-storm, round-robins, rotate roles, defer judgment, idea quotas, cross-pollinate, DACI, Impact/Feasibility Map, pros/cons/ mitigations
Change	CAMPS listening tour, vision statement, simplify the plan, plan early wins, overcommunicate, behavioral cues, normalize change
Development	Capability Mapping, Zoom Out, Venn Zone, IDPs, 3E Model

Mia the Manager

Using the Core BUs and Skills above, our hero – Mia the manager – has come a long way since we first met her. When she started her role as a manager, she felt unsure, overwhelmed, and overworked. Thanks to a lot of reflection, feedback, and practice, she is now self-assured, focused, and building more capacity on her team every day. Luca regularly feels included and finally feels like he's growing. Olivia knows her priorities, works well with other departments, and has a sense of meaning in her work. Kofi is confident in his role, feels like a part of the team, and contributes in creative ways. Mia's manager Alex trusts Mia to involve her at the right times and to make strategic decisions. As a whole, Mia's team members trust one another, have productive meetings, learn quickly thanks to their feedback culture, and are proud to achieve their goals together. All this is the power of great leadership.

Your Leader Lab

Now that we see how Mia and her team have grown, let's reflect on *your* development as a manager since you first started reading this book. Why bother? As you might recall, the best managers we studied weren't born great. They became better faster by **Pausing** to **Extract** their learnings. They owned their own development and saw manager mastery as a continuous pursuit. So, devote a few minutes now to taking the leadership self-assessment you first took at the start of Part II of this book.

Leadership Scenarios Self-Assessment	Score 1–10 (10 = highest)
1. Imagine you have a team member who is demotivated by their work. *How confident are you that you know how to coach them to find more motivation?*	
2. Let's say someone on your team comes across as dismissive when others share ideas. *How confident are you that you know how to give them feedback?*	
3. Assume that one of your team members is constantly overwhelmed, falling behind on deadlines, and having trouble focusing. *How confident are you that you know how to help?*	
4. Effective one-on-one meetings increase engagement, development, and productivity. *How confident are you that you know how to achieve these results with the one-on-ones you have with each person on your team?*	

(continued)

Leadership Scenarios Self-Assessment	Score 1–10 (10 = highest)
5. Imagine that your team is working on a large, complex, cross-functional project. *How confident are you that you know how to help them think strategically and avoid common strategic thinking mistakes?*	
6. Let's say you are leading a meeting where some people are going off topic, some are overtalking, and it's unclear how the group should make a decision. *How confident are you that you know how to course-correct and get the meeting back on track?*	
7. When change happens, team members often resist it or avoid it. *How confident are you that you know how to gain buy-in?*	
8. Assume that one of your team members feels like they are not learning and growing. *How confident are you that you know how to help them develop in ways that are meaningful to them and helpful for the company?*	
9. Great managers know how to leverage their team's diversity, mitigate bias, and make each person feel valued and respected. *How confident are you that you know how to be inclusive?*	
10. Great leaders are also great learners. *How confident are you that you know how to keep learning and growing as a manager?*	
Total leadership confidence score:	

Compare how you scored yourself then and now, and make a big deal out of your progress. To keep on getting better as a manager, schedule a reminder for yourself to review this assessment and the Lab Reports in each chapter of the book at least once a quarter. For live practice, real-time feedback, book club discussion guides, our podcast, and other bonus resources, visit leaderlab.lifelabslearning.com.

We hope you're proud of yourself for the progress you've already made. We know we are. Not only are you making your own life easier and helping your team succeed, you're also becoming a role model of great leadership to others. In this way, you have already joined our mission to help more people become great managers faster.

We wish you many more experiments and adventures in your leader lab!

References

The Backstory

Leone, Paul. 2020. "Measuring the Impact of a Bad Boss." *Training Industry Magazine.* https://www.nxtbook.com/nxtbooks/trainingindustry/tiq_2020 0708/index.php?startid=34#/p/34.

Wigert, Ben, and Jim Harter. 2017. *Re-Engineering Performance Management.* Washington, DC: Gallup Press. https://www.gallup.com/file/workplace/ 238064/Re-EngineeringPerformanceManagement_2018.pdf.

How to Use This Book

Chase, Catherine C., Doris B. Chin, Marily A. Oppezzo, and Daniel L. Schwartz. 2009. "Teachable Agents and the Protégé Effect: Increasing the Effort Towards Learning." *Journal of Science Education and Technology* 18 (June): 334–352. https://doi.org/10.1007/s10956-009-9180-4.

Hewlett, Sylvia A., Melinda Marshall, and Laura Sherbin. 2013. "How Diversity Can Drive Innovation." *Harvard Business Review,* December. https://hbr.org/2013/12/how-diversity-can-drive-innovation.

Part I: The Core BUs
Chapter 1: Q-step

Deci, Edward L., and M. Richard Ryan. 2008. "Self-determination Theory: A Macrotheory of Human Motivation, Development, and Health." *Canadian Psychology/Psychologie canadienne* 49, no. 3 (August): 182–185. https://doi.org/10.1037/a0012801.

Huang, Karen, Michael Yeomans, Alison Wood Brooks, Julia Minson, and Francesca Gino. 2017. "It Doesn't Hurt to Ask: Question-Asking Increases Liking." *Journal of Personality and Social Psychology* 113, no. 3 (September): 430–452. https://doi.org/10.1037/pspi0000097.

Lieberman, Matthew. D., Naomi I. Eisenberger, Molly J. Crockett, Sabrina M. Tom, Jennifer H. Pfeifer, and Baldwin M. Way. 2007. "Putting Feelings into Words: Affect Labeling Disrupts Amygdala Activity in Response to Affective Stimuli." *Psychological Science* 18, no. 5 (May): 421–428. https://doi.org/10.1111/j.1467-9280.2007.01916.x.

Orlob, Chris. "The 7 Best Discovery Call Tips for Sales You'll Ever Read." 2017. Gong, July 5. https://www.gong.io/blog/deal-closing-discovery-call/.

Chapter 2: Playback

Gagné, Robert M., and Ernest C. Smith Jr. 1962. "A Study of the Effects of Verbalization on Problem Solving." *Journal of Experimental Psychology* 63, no. 1 (January): 12–18. https://doi.org/10.1037/h0048703.

Lupyan, Gary, and Daniel Swingley. 2011. "Self-Directed Speech Affects Visual Search Performance." *Quarterly Journal of Experimental Psychology* 65, no. 6 (December): 1068–85. http://dx.doi.org/10.1080/17470218.2011.647039.

Chapter 4: Validate

Amabile, Teresa M., Constance Noonan Hadley, and Steven J. Kramer. 2002. "Creativity Under the Gun." *Harvard Business Review*, August. https://hbr.org/2002/08/creativity-under-the-gun.

Clifton, Jim, and Jim Harter. 2019. *It's the Manager: Moving from Boss to Coach.* Washington, DC: Gallup Press.

Colonial Life. 2019. "Stressed Workers Costing Employers Billions." March 14. https://www.coloniallife.com/about/newsroom/2019/march/stressed-workers-costing-employers-billions.

De Jong, Bart A., Kurt Dirks, and Nicole Gillespie. 2016. "Trust and Team Performance: A Meta-Analysis of Main Effects, Moderators and Covariates." *Journal of Applied Psychology* 101, no. 8 (April): 1134–1150. https://doi.org/10.1037/apl0000110.

Grantcharov, Peter, Thomas Boillat, Sara Elkabany, Katarzyn Wac, and H. Rivas. 2018. "Acute Mental Stress and Surgical Performance. *BJS Open* 3, no. 1 (September): 119–125. https://doi.org/10.1002/bjs5.104.

Green, Charles H., and Andrea P. Howe. 2011. *The Trusted Advisor Fieldbook: A Comprehensive Toolkit for Leading with Trust.* Hoboken, NJ: Wiley.

Van Gennip, Nanine A.E., Mien S.R. Segers, and Harm H. Tillema. 2010. "Peer Assessment as a Collaborative Learning Activity: The Role of Interpersonal Variables and Conceptions." *Learning and Instruction* 20, no. 4 (August): 280–290. https://doi.org/10.1016/j.learninstruc.2009.08.010.

Chapter 5: Linkup

Langer, Ellen, Arthur Blank, and Benzion Chanowitz. 1978. "The Mindlessness of Ostensibly Thoughtful Action: The Role of 'Placebic' Information in Interpersonal Interaction." *Journal of Personality and Social Psychology* 36, no. 6 (June): 635–642. https://doi.org/10.1037/0022-3514 .36.6.635.

Voss, Chris, and Tahl Raz. 2016. *Never Split the Difference: Negotiating as If Your Life Depended on It.* New York: Harper Business.

Chapter 6: Pause

Goleman, Daniel. 2005. *Emotional Intelligence: Why It Can Matter More Than IQ.* New York: Bantam Books.

Gottman, John Mordechai. 1999. *The Marriage Clinic: A Scientifically Based Marital Therapy.* New York: W.W. Norton and Company.

Oppezzo, M., and Daniel L. Schwartz. 2014. "Give Your Ideas Some Legs: The Positive Effect of Walking on Creative Thinking." *Journal of Experimental Psychology: Learning, Memory, and Cognition* 40, no. 4 (April): 1142–1152. https://doi.org/10.1037/a0036577

Trougakos, John P. and Ivona Hideg. 2009. "Momentary Work Recovery: The Role of Within-Day Work Breaks." *Research in Occupational Stress and Well-being* 7, (May): 37–84. https://doi.org/10.1108/S1479-3555(2009)0000007005.

Williams, Jean M., Phyllis Tonymon, and Mark B. Andersen. 1990. "Effects of Life-Event Stress on Anxiety and Peripheral Narrowing." *Behavioral Medicine* 16, no.4: 174–81. https://doi.org/10.1080/08964289 .1990.9934606.

Chapter 7: Extract

Karpicke, Jeffrey D. 2012. "Retrieval-Based Learning: Active Retrieval Promotes Meaningful Learning." *Current Directions in Psychological Science* 21, no. 3 (June): 157–63. https://doi.org/10.1177/0963721412443552.

Klein, Gary. 2007. "Performing a Project Premortem." *Harvard Business Review*, September. https://hbr.org/2007/09/performing-a-project-premortem.

Kruger, Justin, and David Dunning. 1999. "Unskilled and Unaware of It: How Difficulties in Recognizing One's Own Incompetence Lead to Inflated Self-Assessments." *Journal of Personality and Social Psychology* 77, no. 6: 1121–1134. https://doi.org/10.1037/0022-3514.77.6.1121.

Lemoine, C.W. "The Debrief! Fighter Pilot vs. Developer High Aspect BFM DCS Flight (F-5 vs F/A-18)." YouTube video, 27:17. August 19, 2019. https://www.youtube.com/watch?v=M_axdBJnKUM.

Rodgers, Carol. 2002. "Defining Reflection: Another Look at John Dewey and Reflective Thinking." *Teachers College Record* 104 (June): 842–866. http://c21.mcnrc.org/wp-content/uploads/sites/8/2013/05/CarolRodgers-Article.pdf.

Part II: The Core Skills
Chapter 8: Coaching Skills

Casasanto, Daniel, and Angela de Bruin. 2019. "Metaphors We Learn By: Directed Motor Action Improves Word Learning." *Cognition* 182 (January): 177–183. https://doi.org/10.1016/j.cognition.2018.09.015.

Matthews, Gail. 2015. "Goals Research Summary." May. https://braveheart sales.com/wp-content/uploads/Goals-Research-Summary.pdf?x60870.

Nutt, Paul C. 2004. "Expanding the Search for Alternatives during Strategic Decision-Making." *Academy of Management Executive (1993–2005)* 18, no. 4 (November): 13–28. http://www.jstor.org/stable/4166121.

Chapter 9: Feedback Skills

Ashford, Susan J., and Anne S. Tsui. 2017. "Self-Regulation for Managerial Effectiveness: The Role of Active Feedback Seeking." *Academy of Management* 34, no. 2 (November): 251–280. https://doi.org/10.5465/256442.

Bressler, Martin, and Clarence Von Bergen. 2014. "The Sandwich Feedback Method: Not Very Tasty." *Journal of Behavioral Studies in Business* 7 (September): 1–13. http://aabri.com/manuscripts/141831.pdf.

Luna, Tania, and LeeAnn Renninger. 2015. *Surprise: Embrace the Unpredictable and Engineer the Unexpected*. New York: Penguin Trade.

Marks, Stanley W., Joseph Loskove, Andrew Greenfield, Richard E. Berlin, Jennifer Kadis, and Richard Doss. 2014. "Surgical Team Debriefing and Follow-Up: Creating an Efficient, Positive Operating Room Environment to Improve Patient Safety Experience from the Memorial Healthcare System, Florida." *Anesthesia Patient Safety Foundation* 29, no. 1 (June): 1–24. https://www.apsf.org/wp-content/uploads/newsletters/2014/June/pdf/APSF201406.pdf.

Robison, Jennifer. 2006. "In Praise of Praising Your Employees." November 9. https://www.gallup.com/workplace/236951/praise-praising-employees.aspx.

Stone, Douglas, and Sheila Heen. 2014. *Thanks for the Feedback: The Science and Art of Receiving Feedback Well*. New York: Viking Press.

Chapter 10: Productivity Skills

Buehler, Roger, Dale Griffin, and Michael Ross. 1994. "Exploring the "Planning Fallacy": Why People Underestimate Their Task Completion Times." *Journal of Personality and Social Psychology* 67, no. 3 (September): 366–381. https://doi.org/10.1037/0022-3514.67.3.366.

Cirillo, Francesco. 2018. *The Pomodoro Technique: The Acclaimed Time-Management System That Has Transformed How We Work*. New York: Currency, 2018.

Csikszentmihalyi, Mihaly. 2008. *Flow: the Psychology of Optimal Experience*. New York: Harper Perennial Modern Classics.

Gallup. 2017. *State of the Global Workplace*. New York: Gallup Press.

Gino, Francesca, and Bradley Staats. 2016. "Your Desire to Get Things Done Can Undermine Your Effectiveness." *Harvard Business Review*, March 22. https://hbr.org/2016/03/your-desire-to-get-things-done-can-undermine-your-effectiveness.

Gollwitzer, Peter M., and Paschal Sheeran. 2006. "Implementation Intentions and Goal Achievement: A Meta-Analysis of Effects and Processes." *Advances in Experimental Social Psychology* 38 (December): 69–119. https://doi.org/10.1016/s0065-2601(06)38002-1.

Janicik, Gregory A., and Caroline A. Bartel. 2003. "Talking About Time: Effects of Temporal Planning and Time Awareness Norms on Group Coordination and Performance." *Group Dynamics: Theory, Research, and Practice* 7, no. 2 (June): 122–134. https://doi.org/10.1037/1089-2699.7.2.122.

Leinwand, Paul, and Cesare Mainardi. 2011. *Respondents from Firms with Fewer Firm-Wide Strategic Priorities Report Higher Revenue Growth.* January 10. Chart. *Harvard Business Review.* https://hbr.org/2011/04/stop-chasing-too-many-prioriti?registration=success.

Mark, Gloria, Daniela Gudith, and Ulrich Klocke. 2008. "The Cost of Interrupted Work." *Proceeding of the Twenty-Sixth Annual CHI Conference on Human Factors in Computing Systems – CHI '08* (April): 107–110. https://doi.org/10.1145/1357054.1357072.

Masicampo, E. J., and Roy F. Baumeister. 2011. "Consider It Done! Plan Making Can Eliminate the Cognitive Effects of Unfulfilled Goals." *Journal of Personality and Social Psychology* 101, no. 4 (June): 667–83. https://doi.org/10.1037/a0024192.

Pope, Nolan. 2016. "How the Time of Day Affects Productivity: Evidence From School Schedules." *Review of Economics and Statistics* 98, no. 1 (March): 1–11. https://doi.org/10.1162/REST_a_00525.

Rogelberg, Steven G. 2019. *The Surprising Science of Meetings: How You Can Lead Your Team to Peak Performance.* New York: Oxford University Press.

Wieth, Mareike, and Rose Zacks. 2011. "Time of Day Effects on Problem Solving: When the Non-Optimal Is Optimal." *Thinking & Reasoning* 17, no. 4 (March): 387–401. https://doi.org/10.1080/13546783.2011.625663.

Zeigarnik, Bluma. 1938. "On Finished and Unfinished Tasks." In *A Source Book of Gestalt Psychology*, 300–314. Kegan Paul, Trench, Trubner & Company, 1938. https://doi.org/10.1037/11496-025.

Chapter 11: Effective One-on-Ones

Allen, Joseph, Nale Lehmann-Willenbrock, and Nicole Landowski. "Linking Pre-Meeting Communication to Meeting Effectiveness." *Journal of Managerial Psychology* 29, no. 8 (2014): 1064–81. https://doi.org/10.1108/jmp-09-2012-0265.

Amabile, Teresa M., and Steven Kramer. 2011. *The Progress Principle: Using Small Wins to Ignite Joy, Engagement, and Creativity at Work.* Harvard Business Review Press.

Berg, Justin, Jane Dutton, and Amy Wrzesniewski. 2013. "Job Crafting and Meaningful Work." In Bryan J. Dik, Zinta S. Byrne, and Michael F.

Steger (Eds.), *Purpose and Meaning in the Workplace*, pp. 81–104. American Psychological Association https://doi.org/10.1037/14183-005.

Blanchflower, David. 2000. "Self-Employment in OECD Countries." *Labour Economics* 7, no. 5 (September): 471–505. https://doi.org/10.1016/S0927-5371(00)00011-7.

Brewer, Marilynn. B. 1991. "The Social Self: On Being the Same and Different at the Same Time." *Personality and Social Psychology Bulletin* 17, no. 5 (October): 475–482. https://doi.org/10.1177/0146167291175001.

Cable, Daniel M., Francesca Gino, and Bradley R. Staats. 2013. "Breaking Them in or Eliciting Their Best? Reframing Socialization around Newcomers' Authentic Self-Expression." *Administrative Science Quarterly* 58, no. 1 (March): 1–36. https://doi.org/10.1177/0001839213477098.

Clifton, Jim, and Jim Harter. 2019. *It's the Manager: Moving from Boss to Coach.* Washington, DC: Gallup Press.

Cole, Steven W., John P. Capitanio, Katie Chun, Jesusa M. Arevalo, Jeffrey Ma, and John T. Cacioppo. 2015. "Myeloid Differentiation Architecture of Leukocyte Transcriptome Dynamics in Perceived Social Isolation." *Proceedings of the National Academy of Sciences* 112, no. 49 (November): 15142–47. https://doi.org/10.1073/pnas.1514249112.

Corsello, Jason, and Dylan Minor. 2017. "Want to Be More Productive? Sit Next to Someone Who Is." CMCAcorner.Com, February 22. https://cmcacorner.com/2017/02/22/want-to-be-more-productive-sit-next-to-someone-who-is/.

Coupland, Justine. 2003. "Small Talk: Social Functions." *Research on Language and Social Interaction* 36, no. 1: 1–6. https://doi.org/10.1207/S15327973RLSI3601_1.

Dewall, C. Nathan, Geoff MacDonald, Gregory D. Webster, Carrie L. Masten, Roy F. Baumeister, Caitlin Powell, David Combs, et al. 2010. "Acetaminophen Reduces Social Pain: Behavioral and Neural Evidence." *Psychological Science* 21, no. 7 (July): 931–37. https://doi.org/10.1177/0956797610374741.

Eisenberger, Naomi. I., Matthew D. Lieberman, and Kipling D. Williams. 2003. "Does Rejection Hurt? An fMRI Study of Social Exclusion." *Science* 302, no. 5643 (October): 290–292. https://doi.org/10.1126/science.1089134.

Frankl, Viktor E. 1946. *Man's Search for Meaning: An Introduction to Logotherapy.* New York: Touchstone (4th ed., 2000).

Grant, Adam M., Elizabeth M. Campbell, Grace Chen, Keenan Cottone, David Lapedis, and Karen Lee. 2007. "Impact and the Art of Motivation Maintenance: The Effects of Contact with Beneficiaries on Persistence Behavior." *Organizational Behavior and Human Decision Processes* 103, no. 1 (May): 53–67. https://doi.org/10.1016/j.obhdp.2006.05.004.

Hamilton, Barton. 2000. "Does Entrepreneurship Pay? An Empirical Analysis of the Returns to Self-Employment." *Journal of Political Economy* 108, no. 3: 604–631. https://doi.org/10.1086/262131.

Harter, James k., Frank L. Schmidt, Sangeeta Agrawal, Anthony Blue, Stephanie K. Plowman, Patrick Josh, and Jim Asplund. 2020. "The Powerful Relationship Between Engagement at Work and Organizational Outcomes." Gallup. https://www.gallup.com/workplace/321032/employee-engagement-meta-analysis-brief.aspx.

Mann, Annamarie, and Ryan Darby. 2014. "Should Managers Focus on Performance or Engagement?" Gallup.com, August 5. https://news.gallup.com/businessjournal/174197/managers-focus-performance-engagement.aspx.

Moreland, Richard L., and Scott R. Beach. (1992). "Exposure Effects in the Classroom: The Development of Affinity among Students." *Journal of Experimental Social Psychology* 28(3), 255–276. https://doi.org/10.1016/0022-1031(92)90055-O.

Peters, Achim, Bruce S. McEwen, and Karl Friston. 2017. "Uncertainty and Stress: Why It Causes Diseases and How It Is Mastered by the Brain." *Progress in Neurobiology* 156 (September): 164–188. https://doi.org/10.1016/j.pneurobio.2017.05.004.

Rudolph, Cort W., Ian M. Katz, Kristi N. Lavigne, and Hannes Zacher. 2017. "Job Crafting: A Meta-Analysis of Relationships with Individual Differences, Job Characteristics, and Work Outcomes." *Journal of Vocational Behavior* 102 (October): 112–138. https://doi.org/10.1016/j.jvb.2017.05.008.

Schino, Gabriele. 2007. "Grooming and Agonistic Support: a Meta-Analysis of Primate Reciprocal Altruism." *Behavioral Ecology* 18, no. 1 (October): 115–120. https://doi.org/10.1093/beheco/arl045.

Slemp, Gavin, Margaret L. Kern, Kent J. Patrick, and Richard M. Ryan. "Leader Autonomy Support in the Workplace: A Meta-analytic Review." *Motivation and Emotion* 42 (2018): 706–724. https://doi.org/10.1007/s11031-018-9698-y.

Turner, Yehonatan Nizan, and Irith Hadas-Halpern. 2008. "The Effects of Including a Patient's Photograph to the Radiographic Examination." Radiological Society of North America. http://archive.rsna.org/2008/6008880.html.

Wilson, Timothy D., David A. Reinhard, Erin C. Westgate, Daniel T. Gilbert, Nicole Ellerbeck, Cheryl Hahn, Casey L. Brown, and Adi Shaked. 2014. "Just Think: The Challenges of the Disengaged Mind." *Science* 345, no. 6192 (July): 75–77. https://doi.org/10.1126/science.1250830.

Zajonc, Robert B. 1968. "Attitudinal Effects of Mere Exposure." *Journal of Personality and Social Psychology* 9(2, Pt.2), 1–27. https://doi.org/10.1037/h0025848.

Chapter 12: Strategic Thinking

Gamayo, Darde. "Mongoose! The Epic Fail!" 2016. Big Island Now, April 15. https://bigislandnow.com/2016/04/15/mongoose-the-epic-fail/.

Hayes, Jeff, and CPP Global. 2008. "Workplace Conflict and How Businesses Can Harness It to Thrive." CPP Global Human Capital Report. July. https://img.en25.com/Web/CPP/Conflict_report.pdf.

Kabacoff, Robert. 2014. "Develop Strategic Thinkers Throughout Your Organization." *Harvard Business Review*, February 7. https://hbr.org/2014/02/develop-strategic-thinkers-throughout-your-organization.

Mitchell, Deborah J., J. Edward Russo, and Nancy Pennington. 1989. "Back to the Future: Temporal Perspective in the Explanation of Events." *Journal of Behavioral Making* 2, no. 1 (January): 25–38. https://doi.org/10.1002/bdm.3960020103.

Neilson, Gary L., Karla L. Martin, and Elizabeth Powers. 2008. "The Secrets to Successful Strategy Execution." *Harvard Business Review* 86, no. 6 (June): 60–70, 138. https://pubmed.ncbi.nlm.nih.gov/18605030/.

Chapter 13: Meetings Mastery

Bluedorn, A.C., D.B. Turban, and M.S. Love. 1999. "The Effects of Stand-up and Sit-down Meeting Formats on Meeting Outcomes." *American Psychological Association* 84, no. 2 (April): 277–285. https://doi.apa.org/doiLanding?doi=10.1037%2F0021-9010.84.2.277.

Camper, Elaine. 1993. "The Honey Pot: A Lesson in Creativity & Diversity." Glass Insulators Collectors Reference Site. Last modified December 26, 1995. https://www.insulators.info/articles/ppl.htm.

Cohen, Melissa A., Steven G. Rogelberg, Joseph A. Allen, and Alexandra Luong. 2011. "Meeting Design Characteristics and Attendee Perceptions of Staff/Team Meeting Quality." *Group Dynamics: Theory, Research, and Practice* 15, no. 1 (March): 90–104. https://doi.org/10.1037/a0021549.

Doodle. 2019. "The State of Meetings Report." https://meeting-report.com/.

Gawande, Atul. 2009. *The Checklist Manifesto: How to Get Things Right.* New York: Metropolitan Books.

Howard, Jen. 2015. "Clarizen Survey: Workers Consider Status Meetings a Productivity-Killing Waste of Time." Clarizen. January 22. https://www.clarizen.com/press-release/clarizen-survey-workers-consider-status-meetings-a-productivity-killing-waste-of-time/.

Miller, Paddy, and Thomas Wedell-Wedellsborg. 2013. *Innovation as Usual: How to Help Your People Bring Great Ideas to Life*. Boston: Harvard Business Press.

Parnes, Sydney J., and Arnold Meadow. 1959. "Effects of 'Brainstorming' Instructions on Creative Problem Solving by Trained and Untrained Subjects." *Journal of Educational Psychology* 50, no. 4 (August): 171–176. https://psycnet.apa.org/record/1961-02701-001.

Phillips, Katherine W., Gregory B. Northcraft, and Margaret A. Neale. 2006. "Surface-Level Diversity and Decision-Making in Groups: When Does Deep-Level Similarity Help?" *Group Processes & Intergroup Relations* 9, no. 4 (October): 467–482. https://doi.org/10.1177/1368430206067557.

Pope, Nolan G. 2016. "How the Time of Day Affects Productivity: Evidence from School Schedules." *Review of Economics and Statistics* 98, no. 1 (March): 1–11. https://doi.org/10.1162/rest_a_00525.

Rickards, Tudor. 1999 "Brainstorming Revisited: A Question of Context." *International Journal of Management Reviews* 1, no. 1 (March): 91–110. https://doi.org/10.1111/1468-2370.00006.

Rogelberg, Steven G. 2019. *The Surprising Science of Meetings: How You Can Lead Your Team to Peak Performance*. New York: Oxford University Press.

Shiv, Baba, Antoine Bechara, Irwin Levin, Joseph W. Alba, James R. Bettman, Laurette Dube, Alice Isen et al. 2005. "Decision Neuroscience." *Marketing Letters* 16 (December): 375–386. https://doi.org/10.1007/s11002-005-5899-8.

Whetten, David A., and Kim S. Cameron. 1991. *Developing Management Skills* (2nd ed.). New York: HarperCollins.

Wieth, Mareike B., and Rose T. Zacks. 2011. "Time of Day Effects on Problem Solving: When the Non-Optimal Is Optimal." *Thinking & Reasoning* 17, no. 4 (March): 387–401. https://doi.org/10.1080/13546783.2011.625663.

Woolley, Anita Williams, Christopher F. Chabris, Alex Pentland, Nada Hashmi, and Thomas W. Malone. 2010. "Evidence for a Collective Intelligence Factor in the Performance of Human Groups." *Science* 330, no. 6004 (October): 686–688. https://doi.org/10.1126/science.1193147.

Chapter 14: Leading Change

Achor, Shawn. 2010. *The Happiness Advantage: The Seven Principles of Positive Psychology That Fuel Success and Performance at Work*. New York: Broadway Books.

Berwick, Donald M. *Promising Care: How We Can Rescue Health Care by Improving It*. 2014. San Francisco: Jossey-Bass Publishers; 2014.

Blanchard, Ken, John Britt, Judd Hoekstra, and Pat Zigarmi. 2009. *Who Killed Change? Solving the Mystery of Leading People through Change*. New York: HarperCollins Publishers.

Bornstein, Robert F. 1989. "Exposure and Affect: Overview and Meta-Analysis of Research, 1968–1987." *Psychological Bulletin* 106, no. 2: 265–289. https://doi.org/10.1037/0033-2909.106.2.265.

Cummings, Stephen, Todd Bridgman, and Kenneth G Brown. 2015. "Unfreezing Change as Three Steps: Rethinking Kurt Lewin's Legacy for Change Management." *Human Relations* 69, no. 1 (September): 33–60. https://doi.org/10.1177/0018726715577707.

Deutschman, Alan. 2007. *Change or Die: The Three Keys to Change at Work and in Life*. New York: Harper Business.

Fang, Xiang, Surendra Singh, and Rohini Ahluwalia. 2007. "An Examination of Different Explanations for the Mere Exposure Effect." *Journal of Consumer Research* 34, no. 1 (June): 97–103. https://doi.org/10.1086/513050.

Gawande, Atul. 2009. *The Checklist Manifesto: How to Get Things Right*. New York: Metropolitan Books.

Heath, Chip, and Dan Heath. 2010. *Switch: How to Change Things When Change Is Hard*. New York: Random House US.

Kim, Woojong, Yongmin Chang, Jingu Kim, Jeehye Seo, Kwangmin Ryu, Eunkyung Lee, Minjung Woo, and Christopher Janelle. 2014. "An fMRI Study of Differences in Brain Activity Among Elite, Expert, and Novice Archers at the Moment of Optimal Aiming." *Cognitive and Behavioral Neurology* 27, 173–182. doi: 10.1097/WNN.0000000000000042.

Leonardi, Paul M., Tsedal B. Neeley, and Elizabeth M. Gerber. 2011. "How Managers Use Multiple Media: Discrepant Events, Power, and Timing in Redundant Communication." *Organization Science* 23, no. 1 (April 11): 98–117. https://doi.org/10.1287/orsc.1110.0638.

Lewin, Kurt. 1947. "Frontiers in Group Dynamics: Concept, Method and Reality in Social Science; Social Equilibria and Social Change." *Human Relations* 1, no. 1 (June): 5–41. https://doi.org/10.1177/001872674700100103.

Luna, Tania, and Jordan Cohen. 2017. "To Get People to Change, Make Change Easy." *Harvard Business Review*, December 20. https://hbr .org/2017/12/to-get-people-to-change-make-change-easy.

Naples, Michael J. 1979. *Effective Frequency the Relationship between Frequency and Advertising Effectiveness*. New York: Association of National Advertisers.

Sunstein, Cass R., and Richard H. Thaler. 2009. *Nudge: Improving Decisions About Health, Wealth, and Happiness*. New York: Penguin Books.

Chapter 15: People Development

CEB Corporate Leadership Council. 2016. "The New Path Forward." April. https://www.sciencetheearth.com/uploads/2/4/6/5/24658156/2016-04-recursoshumanos4.pdf.

Chase, Catherine C., Doris B. Chin, Marily A. Oppezzo, and Daniel L. Schwartz. 2009. "Teachable Agents and the Protégé Effect: Increasing the Effort Towards Learning." *J Sci Educ Technol* 18 (June): 334–352. https:// doi.org/10.1007/s10956-009-9180-4.

Gartner. 2018. "Managers Can't Be Great Coaches All by Themselves." *Harvard Business Review*. https://hbr.org/2018/05/managers-cant-be-great-coaches-all-by-themselves.

Harter, James k., Frank L. Schmidt, Sangeeta Agrawal, Anthony Blue, Stephanie K. Plowman, Patrick Josh, and Jim Asplund. 2020. *The Relationship Between Engagement at Work and Organizational Outcomes*. Washington, DC: Gallup Press.

Schwartz, Barry. 2004. *The Paradox of Choice: Why More Is Less*. New York: Ecco.

Acknowledgments

Thank you, from the bottom of our hearts to:

Our Labmate editors, for helping us turn our ideas into coherent sentences:

Roi Ben-Yehuda, Rachel Abrahams, Ashley Schwedt, Priscila Bala, and Lea Carey

Our Labmate researchers, for your diligent additions, corrections, and fact-checks:

Roi Ben-Yehuda, Lisa Safran, Alana Burman, Thu-Hang Tran, and Kim Keating

Our book artists, for bringing the whimsy and visual storytelling to this book:

Cat Baldwin (doodles) and Thu-Hang Tran (all other images)

The LifeLabs book development crew, for your wise and wild ideas:

Labmates: *Michelle Wells, Robyn Long, Robleh Kirce, Tiq Milan, Megan Wheeler, Theodore Haber, Victoria Tripsas, Priscila Bala, NeEddra James, Barbie Bowser, Vanessa Tanicien, Ryan Vukelich, Brian Rawson, Zoe Goodman, Massella Dukuly, Rachel Glick, Jamie Nichol, Brendon Nimphius, Li Chen, Abigail Reider, Brian Dann, McKendree Hickory, and Mads Blodgett*

Advisory Team (our Council of Youthful Elders): *Jordan Cohen, Lindsey Dole, Lucy Babbage, Tom Drapeau, Nathan Knight, Matt Hoffman, Cindy Gordon, Cheryl Roubian, Madeline Kolbe Saltzman, Luke Beseda, Lynee Luque, Anju Choudhary, Chrisoula Stassinos, Emanuela Todaro, James Bruce, Natasha Kehimkar, Clare Gobel, Mahlet Getachew, and Missy Ballew*

Our early readers, for your eagle eyes and thoughtful critiques:

Erin Grau, Stien van der Ploeg, Olga Petrova, Lindsey Gilligan, Siri Chilazi, Sam Arpino, Adam Goodman, Joaquín Roca, Dan Manian, Rachel Peck, Lindsey Dole, Tom Drapeau, Alicia Henríquez, Heidi Brooks, Cindy Gordon, Kate Guzik, Coco Brown, Melissa E. Clarke, Alan Cairns, Didier Elzinga, Cheryl Roubian, Brady Donaldson, Chrisoula Stassinos, Luke Beseda, Laurent Schockmel, and Dan Heath.

Our wonderful editor, for nudging us to turn this book into reality and helping us do it well:

Mike Campbell

Our clients and learners, for inspiring us every day with your commitment to transform the workplace into a practice lab for mastering life's most useful skills.

The many managers who joined our research, for allowing us to learn everything we've shared in this book and helping more people become great managers faster.

Author Bios

Tania Luna is the cofounder of LifeLabs Learning. She is a psychology researcher, leadership trainer, and co-author of the book *Surprise: Embrace the Unpredictable & Engineer the Unexpected*. Her work has been featured in dozens of media outlets, including *Psychology Today*, *Harvard Business Review*, TIME, NPR, TED, and *The Wall Street Journal*. She is also the co-host of the podcast *Talk Psych to Me* with her husband, Brian. Tania works, plays, writes, and lives in New York, with her "pack": including her husband, dogs, cat, and pigs.

LeeAnn Renninger, PhD is the cofounder of LifeLabs Learning. She has a doctorate in cognitive psychology, with a specialization in idea transfer and rapid skill acquisition. She launched the content creation and innovation team at LifeLabs Learning, developing the world's best workshops and learning experiences. She is also a researcher, TED speaker, ultramarathoner, Columbia Business School lecturer, and co-author of the book *Surprise: Embrace the Unpredictable & Engineer the Unexpected*.

LifeLabs Learning is the go-to leadership skills accelerator for innovative companies (including Warby Parker, TED, GoPro, Charity:Water, *The New York Times* and 1,000+ others). LifeLabs trains managers, executives, and teams in 'tipping point skills' – small changes that make the biggest impact on engagement and performance – and helps weave these skills into the fabric of company culture.

To keep honing your skills, check out the bonus resources at leaderlab.lifelabslearning.com, and visit LifeLabsLearning.com to bring training to your organization.

Index